M000027882

EX·LIBRIS·

In Advance Praise

Insightful, poignant. Ultimately, genius. One expects this collection of letters to be compulsory reading for any student wishing to enter community college.

~ *The Halifax Weekly Journal*

Can be equally enjoyed by devotees of Jackie Collins and James Joyce.

~ *The Auckland Sun*

The Pavlovas of Butterbrooke Breeze is to literature what dried herring is to the Swedes.

~ *The Helsinki Times-Picayune*

Despite my demanding taping schedule, erecting institutes of education, overseeing my conglomerate, and recommending books such as this one, I simply couldn't put it down. Stedman wept like a schoolgirl.

~ Anonymous

I read it aloud to my fifteen cats. They purred in unison.

~ Mrs Nadine Cooter,
Terre Haute, Indiana,
to *Cat Aficionado*

TPOBB is evidence of the depravity of Western civilization and its ultimate downfall. But Allah save me, I *loved it*. Death to infidels!

~ *The Tehran Free Press*

Loaded with truisms.

~ *Butte Game Hunters Quarterly*

Upon my death, I will bequeath my fortune to one and my copy of this book to another, and I say the latter will be the richer.

~ Seattle Software Mogul

A real page-turner.

~ *Fijian Daily Telegraph*

A gut-wrenching tour de force, propelled by nonstop globe-trotting adventures, not for the faint of heart.

> *~ Summers Dawn Retirement*
> *Community Quarterly Newsletter*

My latest guilty pleasure.

> ~ Sister Maria Elisabeta Lucia,
> St. Salome of the Compelling,
> Sunday Supplement

Industriously composed like a cog in super power wheel.

> *~ People's Republic of Voices*, Beijing

The Pavlovas of Butterbrooke Breeze is more nourishing to the mind, body, and soul than a mother's teat.

> *~ Motorcross Digest*

The Pavlovas of Butterbrooke Breeze

a most curious correspondence

Adderly Harp

The Pavlovas of Butterbrooke Breeze:
A Most Curious Correspondence

Copyright © 2013 Philip Baugh and Olivia Lacson. All rights reserved. No part of this book may be reproduced or retransmitted in any form or by any means without the written permission of the publisher.

Published by Wheatmark®
1760 East River Road, Suite 145, Tucson, Arizona 85718 USA
www.wheatmark.com

ISBN: 978-1-60494-846-2 (paperback)
ISBN: 978-1-60494-857-8 (ebook)
LCCN: 2012943011

This book is
dedicated to

Adderly
Harp

Featured Characters

※ **Sebastian Wentworth Greathead** *(pronounced Grey-Theed)* — *a gentleman*

※ **Countess Cordillia Honeyknob Pryme** — *an aunt*

※ **Giancarlo** — *a groundskeeper*

※ **Manfred Manfred** — *a cook*

※ **Percy** — *a manservant*

※ **Godfrey** — *a manservant*

※ **Brother Ventura** — *a rector*

※ **Charlotte** — *an actress*

※ **Master Smookley, Esq.** — *a solicitor*

※ **Admiral Greathead** — *a father*

※ **Millicent Toastworthy** — *a relation*

※ **Annabelle Toastworthy** — *a child*

※ **Hortence Toastworthy** — *a menace*

※ **Nigel Threadmore** — *an impresario*

※ **Elspeth Stein-Tolkas / Frank** — *an actress*

- ✳ **Captain Toastworthy** — *a husband*

- ✳ **Dr. Basil Carlisle** — *a suitor*

- ✳ **Aldus Tixley** — *a sculptor*

- ✳ **Paulo** — *a groundskeeper*

- ✳ **Prudence Pucklechurch** — *a busybody*

- ✳ **Olivia** — *a trollop*

- ✳ **Spencer Twitmire** — *a solicitor*

- ✳ **Gaston** — *a cook*

- ✳ **Detective Hillary Fingerhinge** — *a constable*

- ✳ **Winifred Wellwater** — *a golfer*

- ✳ **Viscount St. John Pryme** — *a husband*

- ✳ **Dr. Pandosh Kapoor** — *a mystic*

- ✳ **Pippa Higgswallow** — *a cousin*

- ✳ **Sissy Higgswallow** — *a niece*

- ✳ **Prunella Prudeholme** — *a busybody*

- ✳ **Philip** — *a dog*

- ✳ **Ignatius Phinnaeus Toastworthy** — *an infant*

✳ **Mister Barnaby Thaddeus "BT" Rex** — *a Texan*

✳ **Hypsyba** — *a maidservant*

✳ **Jean-Pierre** — *a companion*

✳ **Lorenzo** — *a companion*

✳ **Rosanno** — *a companion*

✳ **Freddie Beverly Winterbottom** — *a companion*

✳ **Sir Ian McElroy** — *a companion*

✳ **Simon Vanfloot** — *a companion*

✳ **Reginald "Strangely" Brown** — *a companion*

✳ **Colin "Cols" Gropewell** — *a companion*

✳ **Trevor Groans** — *a companion*

✳ **George Beadle** — *a companion*

✳ **Charles "Bunny" Chattington** — *a companion*

Chapters

A Matter of a Butterfly Net

1 June
Dear Aunt Cordillia,

It is all in my private journal, which will make fascinating reading one day. Nevertheless, against my customary discretion, I feel compelled to share the wretched details here.

I am of a delicate nature, and my doctor prescribes, if not recommends, utter and complete rest. Therefore, to endure the advances of that brute was, shall I put it, nearly disquieting.

Yes, Aunt, I refer to that swarthy Italian—
and a groundskeeper, no less!

Admittedly, there is no greater pleasure than
enjoying Pavlovas and a complimentary citron
pressé on the south lawn. Whilst I was taking my
refreshments and making entries into my aforementioned journal, that groundskeeper had the
temerity to interrupt my thoughts and invite
me for a frolic amongst the topiary, which, I
will remind, he has neglected since May. Being
a champion of the lower classes, I obliged.

I had thought to bring my trusted butterfly
net along, for the topiary is the home to many
a delightful creature that demands entrap-
ment and examination. But do please inform
your groundskeeper that I am not one of those
creatures.

Well, it is unnamable the things he had in
mind. My butterfly net suffered such injuries
that as a gentleman, I will go no further. I am
afraid it has left a stain on my impressions of

Butterbrooke Breeze. Forgive my audacious straightforward use of the English language, dear Aunt, but I cannot allow a common tradesman to make assumptions about my character.

I Remain Your Loving Nephew,

Sebastian

Wentworth Greathead

(pronounced Grey-Theed)

14 June
Dear nephew,

Take comfort. I have had words with my faithful groundskeeper, Giancarlo, good Giancarlo. You shant be disturbed again. However, I do find it curious that the very day you attest this unfortunate event transpired, I recall how Giancarlo found himself, by your own orchestration, tangled in your butterfly net not once, but three and twenty times that afternoon alone.

Although it has been more than a fortnight, I have been plagued by these peculiar recollections. Then again, my delicate state precludes me from further embellishment. Perhaps an exercise of temperance from the citron *pressé* would prove prudent, considering the circumstances.

I would, nonetheless, suggest ample

servings of Pavlovas, my dear. They have been proven to clarify the mind whilst restoring the soul. I am now well acquainted with my newly acquired cook and his newly invented confectionary delight.

Manfred Manfred comes to me from Bavaria by way of Australia, which I understand is quite a distance from Surrey, from whence I mistakenly believed he originally came. It was all quite a muddle, but just as well. For you see, my darling, had I known his true origin, it is doubtful he would have made entry within the forecourt, much less the inner sanctum of Butterbrooke Breeze. And, alas, I would have never known the wonder that is the Pavlova.

My manservant, Percy, tells me that the Pavlova receives its name from the famed Russian prima ballerina whom Manfred Manfred struck quite the acquaintance whilst in confinement, I believe was the word Percy used, at a Sydney workhouse. Manfred had once dreamed of taking the stage himself, but considering his stature, dancing *en pointe* was ill advisable.

These details are fatiguing to your aunt, but Manfred has shown he is capable and will remain in my employ as long as the Pavlovas remain unperjurable.

As of good Giancarlo, he has hence been ineffectual of late. Pity, I daresay my prized topiaries have suffered the worst of it.

Cordially,
Aunt Cordillia

21 June
Dearest Aunt Cordi,

Would you mind if I address you by your pet name? Godfrey only just delivered your recent missive to me in my bedchamber. It is known that you enjoy your occasional sherry before elevenses, but I believe you must have Giancarlo confused with the Rector, Brother Ventura, from Butterbrooke Abbey.

Ventura and I did indeed take a restful stroll amongst the gardens, but nothing as untoward as a butterfly net was employed.

Godfrey has brought me a sleep draught and drawn a bath. This afternoon has been far too taxing. It is my hope the dreadful Giancarlo will attend to his duties henceforth.

This event reminds of the time I mistakenly traveled to Naples alone. It is all in my journal, and should I expire prematurely, you will find it very interesting reading.

Your adoring nephew,

Sebastian

23 June
Dearest Basty,

Perhaps my recollections betray me. Odd, your vehement protestations, "Giancarlo, you may not take your leave from my butterfly net until you prune my shrubbery!" may have been misinterpreted. You have plainly communicated your distaste for Giancarlo, good Giancarlo. And yet he felt compelled, as if specifically instructed, to tend your garden. The language barrier must be at fault.

Thankfully, one can soak their troubles in a sleep draught. As for Brother Ventura, yes, he has been inclined to find himself entangled in your butterfly net as well.

It calls to mind a time when both Ventura and Giancarlo emerged from the rectory quite disheveled followed by you, my dear nephew. Curious …

Clever of you to possess more than one net in your arsenal! As for your Naples adventure, like my topiaries, it shant ever recover.

Your most dubious aunt,
Cordillia

26 June

Sweet, dearest Aunt C,

I will allow your misapprehensions due to your many odd years in widowhood with little more than your hours at the loom to beguile the tedium that comprises your existence. I cannot abide, however, your implication that Brother Ventura would offer me anything other than conversation of a purely ecclesiastical nature.

What I could *possibly* have in common with a groundskeeper with dark, dirty, calloused hands who spends his wages at the Bull & Boar is beyond my imagination! The next time I write will be from the Café de Flore in the St. Germain des Pres. My physician recommends a change of scenery, but Paris weather is so changeable.

Adieu,

Basty

30 June
My darling boy!

Your humour is absolutely *charming*! How you do delight this aged dowager so. You astutely mentioned my whiling away my tedium conjuring "misapprehensions," did you say?

If by misapprehensions you mean perfectly transcribed passages of your journal that explicitly depict in every illicit detail your rompings, however ecclesiastic they may have been, with the Rector, not to mention good Giancarlo, perhaps I misconstrued the aforementioned events.

My dear nephew, you may have not been aware that I recently intercepted your correspondence directed to my illiterate groundskeeper, exalting the very dark, dirty, calloused hands you find so appalling.

Well, despite the notarized confirmation that this letter amongst a sheaf of other letters was penned by you, my little scuttlebutt, perhaps these are merely the imaginings of an old woman. *C'est la vie.*

Please extend my love to Charlotte, and do remind her to return my tiara. I have no appropriate adornments for the last Thursday of each month.

Kisses of heaven!
Auntie Cordi

4 July

Dear Aunt Cordillia,

It has been ages since I last received word from you. Has your arthritis been plaguing you again? I pray not, as it would prevent you from enjoying the better part of the day at the loom.

I regret to say Jean-Pierre turned out not to be a credit to his race, if you call the French "a race," and I certainly do. He had some disquieting habits that decorum prevents me from addressing in detail here.

Upon reflection, the Neapolitan townespeople were friendly and accommodating. I have thrown caution to the wind and decided to give Naples another go and will be spending the remainder of the month there, then may make a mad dash to Mykonos before the rush of "tourists" from America.

Pray write soon if your ailments will allow. Even now, I can picture your gnarled rheumatoidal hands clasped together in prayer. Perhaps you could dictate to Percy. He is seventy-seven but still might be helpful.

Yours devoted,

Sebastian

A Misunderstanding in Naples

11 July
Dear Aunt Cordillia,

It is grape-stomping season, and the Chianti bottles cannot be filled fast enough. My *nuovo amico*, Lorenzo, has invited me for a picnic and an intriguing game of his own invention. Let us just say that I very much doubt these grape stains can be removed from my summer seersucker. It might be best if Godfrey simply takes a match to it and we go into towne for a new ensemble.

Your old neighbour, Prudence Puckle-church, is abroad and has unfortunately taken rooms at my *pensione*. She keeps popping in uninvited. I was just about to make an entry into my private journal when she requested from me a list of my favourite French poets. What she has up her garishly embroidered sleeve, I fear to conjecture.

Arrivederci,

Your nephew

14 July
My dear little Basty,

My, it is good to hear from you at last! After days of limited correspondence, I feared you may have gone ill or taken with the gypsies again. I was beside myself with grief. My poor nerves! If not for the consistent medicinal applications by my faithful manservant, Percy, and the delightful musings of good Giancarlo, I suspect my vapours would have consumed me.

Giancarlo, although still not fully recovered from those unfortunate events of many weeks past (I am still quite put out over the whole matter!), informs me that, alas, Mellon Ball Grange is finally let. It has been ages since Butterbrooke Breeze has had the detriment of neighbours. We have not yet ascertained the identity of these interlopers, but that shall all be sussed out shortly.

19

Presently, I have resigned myself to my loom. My *loom of gloom*, as Percy's uncensored nocturnal admissions once betrayed. There are, of course, my daily jaunts to Butterbrooke Abbey to soothe the spirits. You will be pleased to know that the Rector is well and sends his greetings. I made mention of your extended holiday to Naples. He warns of the last time you found yourself grape stained, with scandalous results.

My dear nephew, I entreat you to please take care. See that Godfrey sets your suit ablaze straightaway. Better not to save the incrimination, my dear. Now as for Prudence, that shrew of a woman! It would be best to stay clear from the likes of her. Now pray, write soon, dear nephew. You know your aunt has little of entertainment.

Do behave,

Aunty Cordillia

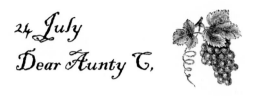

24 *July*
Dear Aunty C,

It was wonderful to read your latest missive. I expect to return to the halls of Butterbrooke Breeze before the first leaf turns gold. If I may impose upon your graces, I would adore it if you be so kind as to weave me an aubergine cravat on the loom.

I found the most divine clothier in Naples. Rosanno is his name. He took my measurements over a period of several days to ensure my latest seersucker fits my form, and I believe an aubergine cravat would complement nicely. However, I fear I must return home soon, as the constant diet of pasta is doing nothing for my waistline. The seersucker becomes ever so snug.

I read your notations concerning Giancarlo. My kindness of heart and good Christian disposition compels me to forgive his peculiar habits. One must absolve him, as he is only human. Like his gardening trousers, we all fall short of the glory of God, as they say. He is not the first common tradesman to forget his place when in my presence. I will have to invite him for tea upon my return.

Your loving,

Basty

6 August
Dearest Basty,

Imagine my surprise and delight that no sooner than a fortnight I should receive a letter from you, my dear boy! Please do not tease your poor aunt with promises of a visit, but one does hope you will honour your aunt with your company. You are most welcome.

As for good Giancarlo, let us call a truce, shall we? Nay, we shan't speak of those unfortunate events again.

I am pleased to learn your newfound clothier has fashioned you a suit. I presume that Godfrey has disposed of its predecessor most discretely. Your man, Rosanno, is it? Well, I suppose days and days of measurements are to be expected, particularly for a renowned clothier. That inseam, as you are very much aware, can prove such a challenge.

It reminds me of when you were a mere lad, fascinated with your dear dead mama's measuring tape. When it no longer served its true purpose, oh how you would measure, gauge, and cipher this and that. Quite fixated you were with length and girth. It was quite the task removing that seamstress tool from your stout little hands.

Oh, such memories. Do come soon! You have my most solemn of vows that Giancarlo, good Giancarlo, will be restricted to the topiary garden.

Safe journeys my sweet boy,
Aunt Cordillia

11 August
Dear Aunt C,

Thank you for your warm letter. I have decided to shorten my trip to Naples for reasons too numerable to mention. First-class accommodations to Southampton were not to be found. To my dismay, a clerk offered to settle me in steerage!

Fortunately, a strapping young gentleman named Freddie Winterbottom overheard my dilemma and offered that I should bunk with him over the long passage across the Mediterranean, around the Iberian Peninsula, and finally back to civilization in the Isles. As it turns out, Freddie is a coxswain on the Oxford rowing team. That is pronounced *cocks-sin*, for your elucidation.

I expect my train to arrive at Butterbrooke Station on the twentieth at twenty-two minutes after four in the afternoon. Please send Percy round with the carriage, won't you? My journey should prove quite exhausting, and I look forward to mounds of reparative Pavlovas. Perhaps you could invite the kindly Rector, Brother Ventura?

Missing you terribly,

awfully, horribly,

Your Basty

18 August
My dear, dear Basty,

The news of your homecoming does your poor old aunt a world of good. I already have Percy positioned at the station in anticipation of your arrival. Terrible inconvenience, having to bunk with that coxswain. Although I appreciate the pronunciation, I am quite familiar with the term.

I believe Percy himself once wore the title proudly and still does from time to time.

Do not fret. I shall have an assortment of scrumptious confections for your consumption. I may even tempt you with bites of Pavlovas, but only if you promise to behave yourself, my incorrigible little sprite.

You are welcome to invite Master Winter-bottom to tea. The Rector has already promised

27

to be in attendance. I clasp my frail hands in glee!

Yours most devotedly,

Aunt Cordillia

18 August
Dearest
Sebastian, **STOP**

You find your aunt exceptionally disturbed. **STOP** Percy has just placed before me a news clipping anonymously sent from Naples. **STOP** This article, to my dismay, cites you, my dear Basty, as a person of interest regarding a dreadful incident involving the corruption of three Italian youths and the desecration of a most beloved fountain. **STOP** Hurry home, my dear boy. **STOP** We must have this sorted straight away. **STOP** What will the neighbours say? **STOP** My poor nerves! **STOP**

Distressed, **STOP**
Aunt Cordillia **STOP**

18 August

Dear Aunt C, **STOP**

All a misunderstanding regarding said youths and fountain. **STOP** Nonetheless, Naples *polizia* easily bribed. **STOP** Arriving at Butterbrooke tomorrow after next. **STOP** Prepared to sojourn a fortnight. **STOP** Freddie of Oxford rowing team wants me to join him at Leamington on Thames. **STOP** Ta! **STOP** With an extra helping of Ta! **STOP**

SWG **STOP**

1 September
Dear Aunt C,

Since I will be arriving later than originally planned due to circumstances involving my passport and its temporary seizure, it would be my honour, if your calendar permits, to take you to luncheon on the High Street tomorrow. You have been only too kind as an aunt and my trusted friend. There is a quaint tearoom that is all the rage. I believe it is called Tarts, named for its unparalleled desserts and waitstaff. Godfrey could transport us in my carriage into towne. I look forward to learning about your latest project at the loom. Were you not knitting a burial shroud for the Widow fforbes-Hamilton? Poor dear. She was so sharp right up to the end.

Undyingly yours,
Sebby

6 September
Dear Nephew,

Yes, tea in towne would be quite lovely. But, Nephew, something alarming has been brought to my attention. Moments after Percy posted my correspondence to you, a solicitor presented him a summons from the Italian courts demanding your presence at a hearing scheduled not a month from today. It made mention of the three Italian youths!

This is all too distressing! I can scarcely complete my knitting today, never mind my weaving. Widow fforbes-Hamilton will just have to go shroudless. Percy insists I postpone any further inquiry until our tea tomorrow. Oh, my dear Basty, what is there to do? Perhaps Pavlovas and citron *pressé* will calm the nerves.

Until tomorrow, my dear!
Aunt Cordillia

7 September
Dear Aunt Cordi,

Oh dear, that *is* most alarming! I scarcely care to spend another night in the Neapolitan police station. It was filled to the bursting point with all varieties of Italians. Frankly, the entire city was overrun with them. I am not one to say a particular race of people has certain inclinations, but by and large, Italians seem to live only for the day and live in rank dissipation with unhealthy appetites of excess on every level. It is much incongruous to what I am accustomed to, to be sure.

Perhaps it might be best to forgo our little

luncheon and rather not return to Butter-brooke straightaway. I might assume *persona non grata* and remain incognito, so to speak, and call upon Freddie Winterbottom until this inconvenience subsides. What I would do for clouds of Pavlovas at this very moment. Well, nevertheless …

Toodle pip and a hearty ta!

S

10 September

Dear Basty,

If you think it best. However, I am quite put out. I do long for an extended visit from my dear nephew. Let us partake of Pavlovas until we are ill with delight at another time.

Percy advises that perhaps a stay with your coxswain would be best. For being a coxswain, my, if he is not accommodating! I will resign myself to a leisurely tea alone at my loom.

Much subdued,

Aunt Cordillia

16 September

Dear Aunt C,

I knew you would understand if anyone would. I remember you telling me how you found yourself in a few scrapes in your day. Did you not once cause quite the scandal when you arrived for vespers with red riding gloves and without a hat?

This will all blow over soon, as is always the case with me. Then I, and perhaps Winterbottom, will return to your bosom. (I speak metaphorically, naturally.) Freddie showed great signs of hospitality, and he thinks I will make quite a splash with his teammates. (I speak aquatically, naturally.)

Must splish,

Basty

20 September
Dearest Basty,

What a pleasure to take tea with your companion Master Winterbottom, however brief it was! I daresay the High Street has not enjoyed such regality. Your Winterbottom has all the warmth of high summer. So attentive he must be to you, my dear nephew. He reminded me of Mama's Bulgarian lap dog, Bonaparte.

Master Winterbottom did extend your regrets. I understand the chilblains can weaken even the most stalwart of young men.

But Basty, what a peculiar coincidence! Not long after my luncheon with Master Winterbottom, who should turn up at Butterbrooke, but that mealy-mouthed solicitor? He was quite insistent on speaking with you despite my protestations. Alas, to prove once and for all you were not seeking refuge at Butterbrooke, I felt compelled to ask him to join us for tea. My water closet has never seen so much activity.

He introduced himself as Master Smookley, Esq., London. Apparently, he was employed by the Naples Towne Council of sorts to seek you out. Evidently, the townespeople are still quite upset about their befouled fountain. Oh, and of course the three Italian youths. He disclosed his plan of traveling to your father's autumnal estate, Waverly Point, to inquire after you there. I cannot tell you how flutterings of distress nearly consumed me.

After a time, and seven servings of Pavlovas later, he expressed some satisfaction and mentioned an interest in my garden. Giancarlo, good Giancarlo, offered to escort him round my prized topiaries and of course the regaled potting shed. You know, my dear Basty, following their extensive tour, Master Smookley relented. He accepted payment of seventy-five crown for the repair of the befouled fountain and went on his way.

Dear Basty, is that not wondrous news? At last, you may visit your aunt unencumbered by the burden of discovery. Well, I am called away to my archery lesson. Please extend my greetings to Master Winterbottom. You are both welcome at Butterbrooke Breeze.

I expect you home soon,

Aunt Cordillia

24 September

Dear treasured Aunt C,

I am fairly giddy with joy upon hearing this gay news! I am not entirely surprised at how easily Master Smookley, Esq., yielded after payment of seventy-five crown and a thorough tour of the potting shed. You have gone above and beyond the duties of an aunt. And Giancarlo! Great Giancarlo has dug low and deep in his duties as a groundskeeper. Then to send Smookley on his merry way with a stomach filled to the bursting with Pavlovas is gastronomic judiciousness.

I can no longer be denied of my own portion of Pavlovas. You should find me at Butterbrooke as early as this Saturday. Although Freddie has a few more points of interest to show me, I will have to leave Master Winterbottom behind, as rowing season has begun and his duties as coxswain come first.

Winterbottom is indeed a fine chap. His teammates are equally generous and eager to show me round Royal Leamington Spa. Freddie expressed to me how wonderful it must be to have a kind, loving aunt who will stop at nothing to ensure my happiness. I look forward to a long and restful stay at Butterbrooke after this somewhat trying period.

Naples! It may be a long time indeed before I venture back to that barbaric country. I must think of a way to repay your kindness as well as that of Giancarlo's. Perhaps I judged him too harshly …

I was at the booksellers' this weekend and picked up a yellowed copy of *A Saturday Life* by Radclyffe Hall, one of the most celebrated authors of the day. Her tendencies are a matter of public record. I will read it on the train and share it with you soon. That is, if you have any interest in reading the works of this self-confessed paramour of the linguistic arts.

I must dash, as Freddie wants me to assist in honing his coxswain skills this very afternoon. See you on Saturday! Please send Percy twenty-three minutes after six in the evening at Butterbrooke Station. I will require reparative Pavlovas after my lengthy journey.

Your grateful nephew,

SWG

25 September
Dear Aunt Cordillia,

My arrival at Butterbrooke will be delayed
due to circumstances beyond my control. My
dear chum, Freddie Winterbottom has been
sent to hospital after their *canoe*, I believe it
is called, overturned. I was cheering them
on from the banks of the river. Poor Freddie
became distracted. They rowed starboard
instead of port. All swam safely to shore, save
my dear Freddie, who floundered, well … like
a flounder. I think whisking him off to hospital
was a textbook case of overreaction. Only
Freddie's pride was injured in the incident.
He failed to see the humour in the situation,
as his coxswain horn sank into the depths of
the river, of course. Let us just say it has put a
damper on our friendship.

I anticipate with glee the idea of visiting my dear aunt for much needed rest and relaxation. My private journal demands updating. A good many tales I will write in it, too. Until the morrow!

Your loving,
Basty

2 October
Dearest Basty,

'Tis unfortunate about Master Winterbottom. A drowned horn is something to be mourned.

Yet what gorgeous news! I clasp my hands in arthritic joy! All of Butterbrooke is elated at the prospect of your return. We shall indulge ourselves in Pavlovas galore. I have already installed Percy at the train station in anticipation of your arrival. Giancarlo, good Giancarlo, is secured in the potting shed. The Rector has been alerted and has confirmed he shall come to tea. All is prepared for your homecoming, my little cherub.

By the by, do not be alarmed, but your father, Admiral Greathead, in a recent correspondence made mention his plans of traveling to Royal Leamington Spa for a bit of recreation and of course to see you, my dear boy. Shall I send word letting him know of your plans to return to Butterbrooke? For if it is recreation he desires, no activity on earth can rival the sea bathing to be had at Butterbrooke Breeze. As well you know, it is esteemed in exalted circles as the modern Bath for those of a discriminating palate. Oh, what diversion to have both my dear nephew and the great Admiral Greathead as my esteemed guests!

I shall look forward to your arrival presently,
Aunt Cordillia

6 October

Dear Aunt C,

I am answering your letter post-haste. Regarding my father, the admiral, like Freddie's coxswain horn, do you ever have the sinking feeling I am somewhat of a disappointment to Father? I mean, matriculating from one military school to the next must have been a sabre to his side, although I **did** make a great many friends there. My interests in The Arts seems to dismay the admiral. I gather he carried other hopes for his only son.

I am pleased the Rector will be round for tea. A man of the cloth may subdue Father's mood. I can only pray that Giancarlo will remember his station and not venture too far from the potting shed.

Come to think of it, my salivary glands are fairly moist with anticipation of Manfred's famed Pavlovas.

Toodle with an extra pip!

Basty

10 October
Dearest Nephew,

This is not meant to be harsh, but of course you are and always have been a disappointment to your dear papa. What would make you think otherwise? His displeasure with you has been well established. However, you, my dear boy, have excelled in ways that would not have been possible without the admiral's disapproval. The townespeople of Naples can attest to that.

Take comfort, the admiral seeks fault in all. Condescension is elemental to his charm. How insufferable he was last summer, critically examining my topiaries! So, you see, I am completely empathetic to your position.

Oh, how wonderful it will be to have two formidable forces at Butterbrooke for a bit of amusement. Perhaps Giancarlo might be released from the potting shed to enhance the entertainment. As you can well imagine, the loom possesses limited pleasure. Do not fret about the admirable admiral. Assuredly, all will be well.

Yours most supportively,
Aunt Cordillia

14 October
Dear Auntie,

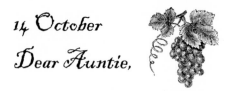

It is ironic Father would cast doubts upon your prized shrubbery when he insists on nurturing that follicle growth that began above his lip and which has now crawled down each jowl.

As my good fortune would have it, I can thank my dear mama, God rest her soul, for instilling in me the appreciation for "The Arts" and all its aesthetic values.

I hope Father does not challenge me to a game of croquet. I do not wish to encourage perspiration.

Pavlovas at eight then,

S

19 October
Dearest Seb,

You are quite right about your papa's facial shrubbery. It is in need of a vigorous pruning. A tidier facial arrangement would suit him well. Perhaps Giancarlo could render his services? The admiral has yet to refuse my Giancarlo. But like Manfred, your father may cleave onto his hirsuteness.

Please do not forget that as your most faithful, dearest relation, I have always admired your artistic abilities. Your dear, dead mama, an appreciator of many things, not the least of which aesthetic, may heaven keep her soul, was not alone on that account. Speaking of the aesthetic, my nearest surroundings will be blessed by the sight of you soon. And I just received word that the admiral will indeed be joining our little party.

Most delighted!

Auntie C

23 October
Dear Aunt C,

I am sorry to have to beg off this trip. Dear father means well, but he continues to suggest that I should assume a more vigorous activity than horizontals on my holiday. He often looks at me with scorn through his monocle, a sort of one-eyed squint, if you will. Also, as much as I adore your sister-in-law, Millicent Toastworthy, I simply cannot abide her five-year-old twins, Annabelle and Hortence. Where they adopted the idea of running up and kicking me in the shins as amusement, I shall never know. I will not have *MYYY* holiday impaired by unruly tots.

Do you remember my friend Charlotte, the actress in experimental theatre? She and her actor friends are reviving the drama *What the Butler Saw* at the Haymarket. They have asked me to read the part of the corpse.

My character is relegated to few lines, mutterings actually, but it is a foot, an albeit decomposed one, in the door of legitimate theatre, which I always felt was my true calling.

The admiral will be pleased that I am earning an honest wage, even if it is for amusement. For the time being, I have taken a flat with the young man who is mounting this theatrical offering, as my own abode undergoes renovations. Did I not write that Back Passage is being fitted with a new backsplash? You can write me in care of Nigel Threadmore, III, at 14 Penwiper Mews, Knightsbridge, London, SW1.

Nigel received his training in dramatics whilst working in a traveling trapeze troupe. He is quite … nimble.

And thus I am certain this play will enjoy a long run. Perhaps you may come to towne and see me. I have not seen any reviews on my performance, but my fellow thespians assure

me that I am most believable as a corpse. Ta
and cuddles!

Yours cadaverously,

Basty

31 October
Dearest Nephew,

Oh how I long for your return to my metaphorical bosom. Your visit would do a continent of good. Alas, our reunion was once again aborted. After a day of Toastworthys, this is an idea Millicent Toastworthy should have considered six years ago.

I daresay your father was quite peevish at your absence. His monocle so fogged over in his vexations that it took Giancarlo hours of spirited rubbings to clear it. Now I am quite alone. My loom has not seen so much activity since your leave-taking as many months ago.

Am I to understand, darling nephew, your intent for a career on the stage? But, my dear, how will you cope? You have always been a gentleman of no profession. You must be careful not to quit the sphere of influence to that of which you have been bred. Oh, what your father will say!

Well, my little cherished one, I have fashioned the enclosed waistcoat to combat London's variable weather.

Felicitations & remonstrations,
Aunt Cordillia

4 November

Dear Aunt C,

Oh, but I do love my new waistcoat. It is quite fetching and has generated an undo amount of jealousy amongst my fellow thespians. Thank you very much, indeed! Your thoughtful consideration of the placement of vertical stripes is too kind. I think of your poor, gnarled, arthritic hands working piously at the loom for hours upon ceaseless hours, peering over the south lawn in the perpetual solitude that is Butterbrooke.

As it is no surprise, the play was a resounding success. Reviews have been raving, and it will be taken on the road to Brighton. Sadly, since theatrical triumph was achieved, Nigel has rejoined the traveling trapeze troupe, which was fairly unlucky now that they have relinquished the net.

I did befriend the benefactor of the theatre

guild, who asked me to organize his papers. He is generously putting me up at his lovely home in Sloane Square, Mayfair. Future correspondence may be sent care of Sir Ian McElroy, Pembrooke, #2 Sloan Square, London, SW2.

Perhaps you are acquainted with Sir Ian? He thinks he attended Eaton at the same time as your late husband. I must dash, as Sir Ian had invited me for cocktails at the Savoy.

Cheers,

SWG

Manfred the Bavarian

Sebastian Wentworth Greathead, Thespian
c/o Nigel Threadmore, III
14 Penwiper Mews
Knightsbridge, London, SW1

FORWARDED TO

Sebastian Wentworth
Greathead, Thespian
c/o Sir Ian McElroy
Pembrooke
#2 Sloan Square,
London, SW2

12 November
Dearest Nephew B,

I am overjoyed you are fond of the waistcoat. The paisley polka-dotted pattern with vertical stripes is not too modern for your theatre colleagues? You are quite right in assuming that it was an arduous task for my frail hands. These untold years have been unkind to my rheumatism.

Come to think of it, there is no greater remedy for my various ailments than a holiday. You mentioned that your troupe might be bearing towards Brighton? Lovely! I believe I shall meet you and your artistic companions there.

I do look forward to seeing you, my sweet Basty, in your debut! You were always so accomplished at playing dead as a child. I remember how we nearly put to ground when you were not one and seven years! What a chuckle that caused.

I will alert Percy at once. Giancarlo, good Giancarlo, shall remain behind to mind Butterbrooke Breeze. However, I shall include Manfred as an escort. Come to find out, Manfred is actually a *she*. Although, her Bavarian carriage, husky tenor, and mannish hands are quite convincing to the contrary.

Oh what Pavlovas Manfred has conjured these last days! I believe they will well prove effective in luring you back to Butterbrooke. I shall forward you the particulars of my Brighton holiday soon. Until then, be good!

Yours most confectionately,
Aunt Cordillia

16 November

Dearest Aunt C,

How intriguing that Manfred turned out in actuality to be a *fräulein*. I have an actress friend I should introduce her to, Elspeth Stein-Toklas, but she prefers to be addressed as Frank. Frank decided to step out of the spotlight and is more in her element when constructing sets and whatnot. I have never seen a woman brandish a hammer with such alacrity.

The sea air would do you good, Aunt. A quiet diversion from your otherwise tedious existence at the loom.

As for me, I am unsure if this acting bug has bitten as I once thought. I long for something more, something more dynamic than simply lying there playing dead. Often I have envied old school chums like Simon Van Floot, who discovered his calling in the dynamic world of insurance underwriting with Lloyds. Perhaps you are right: I was simply not meant for the workaday world. I just hope Father never decides to cut off funds.

Charlotte is nipping over to Paris and thinks I require exposure to, that is to say, "The Arts." But what have I been employed in these last few months? She is certain I would become fast friends with some of the fellows in the Ballet Francaise. No doubt that is true, as I am so genial. Additionally, I consider myself an ambassador of goodwill for Her Royal Highness. Wherever I go, so goes England. I care to deport myself accordingly at all times.

Perhaps several weeks at Butterbrooke will clear my head. I have quite forgiven Giancarlo and found a side to him (I cannot recall which one) that is actually quite pleasant, even if he is not a sparkling conversationalist.

Pray the twins do not return. Annabelle and Hortence are the most bothersome children. Is it true that Millicent Toastworthy is with child yet again? *Oh dear.* I gather we both know what that entails! Yes, you will be charged with another celebration. I will assist you with the fete this one last time, dear aunt, but only because I adore you and owe you a debt of gratitude for sorting out of that slippery situation with the Neapolitan *polizia*. But really, these festivities must stop. I cannot be expected to run out and procure a christening gown every times she sneezes!

Must dash again. There is a special drinks party tonight at the home of Sir Ian. It is Elspeth's, pardon me … *Frank's* birthday.

For she's a jolly good fellow,

Basty

20 November
Dearest Basty,

Perhaps, when we are in Brighton, Manfred and Frank might be introduced. However, that may be unlikely, since Manfred is perpetually engaged in concocting the curious confectionary delight that is the Pavlova day and night. Poor dear. Manfred has not the time to even mind her toilet, and her hirsute chin has gone neglected for weeks.

My excitement towards my holiday grows daily. Although I am surrounded by the sea, since Butterbrooke Breeze, as you may recall, my darling nephew, overlooks the treacherous channel, I long for the foreign waters of Brighton.

You mention your shriveling interest, this time in a career on the stage. My fickle little cherub! I do hope your weariness may be allayed until I have the opportunity to see my nephew in all his deceased glory. Basty, please be sure to reserve a box for your auntie!

As for that nuisance of a woman Millicent, my how perceptive you are! Perhaps you missed your true calling as a soothsayer or midwife or as a soothsaying midwife? Yes, yes, she may be with child yet again. Oh, what my dead husband would say to his dead brother's wife! I have refused outright to organize any manner of celebrations for her next litter.

You have reminded me of Hortence and Annabelle. I have not told you how they nearly spoilt my prized topiaries. Giancarlo was inconsolable in their terrible wake. I nearly set Manfred to them, but Millicent's screeching protestations persuaded me to simply turn them out.

Now, do not fret, dear nephew. As sure as his unkempt whiskers, the admiral has no intention of cutting you off. At any rate, in a few years you will be coming into your mother's fortune, which was acquired at great cost to one's reputation.

As long as you continue to carry yourself with the comportment that is expected of your position, you will be well received in the company of the most dignified members of society. Why, even good Giancarlo made mention of how well you have improved. But seeing that he does not speak nor understand the Queen's English, he might well have been commenting on the quality of our soil. Dear, simple bronzed creature!

Take care not to gobble too much of Elspeth's, or was it Frank's, cake, when there are Pavlovas to be had! By the by, I shall be arriving at Brighton station eleven after five in the evening. Please do have porters at the ready near the first-class coach. That's a dear.

Yours ever faithfully,
Aunt Cordillia

25 November

Dear Aunt C,

Of course, how silly of me. Butterbrooke Breeze does indeed overlook the treacherous channel. But Brighton carries the less imposing waters which makes dipping into it that much less intimidating. It is the devil in me speaking, but often I wished the five-year-old twins would attempt a channel crossing by doing the Australian crawl. Next time, I may dare them.

I look forward to your arrival in Brighton! We must have high tea at the Breakers. And there is a yarnery just off the High Street that may hold some interest for you. It adjoins the Royal British Loom Museum, another point of interest not to be missed!

I have come to know a young pastry chef there by the name of Reginald Browne, but everyone here calls him "Strangely." True, his ancestry is uncertain. He may very well originate from Tunisia, but then, I never considered Tunisia the real Africa, do you?

Be that as it may, I have personally sampled his scones. In fact, I am partaking of one as I pen this. I do not exaggerate when I say he has the most savory scones south of Tenley of Thames.

Licking the crumbs in rhapsody,

Basty

30 November
Dearest Nephew B,

Millicent is once again insisting on bringing her brood for another visit. Can you fathom it, my dear Basty? As I mentioned before, she is expecting! We may not take her as a wit, but she is as fertile as the Nile Delta.

My, how we two think so well alike! I was just this moment toying with the idea of encouraging the twins with sleep-elixir-laced Pavlovas, then on to a brief channel excursion on Percy's dinghy. Impish thought, I know. They are both so fond of sailing. It must be bred into them from their lecherous father, Captain Toastworthy. If they call during my holiday, Giancarlo, good Giancarlo, will see to them.

I look forward to your company and high

tea at the Breakers. It sounds delightful. I am intrigued to be introduced to your Tunisian acquaintance Master Strangely Browne. You are quite right. Tunisia, though not quite the Congo, might be considered to be of the Middle Eastern or perhaps of the Spanish connection, but it is most certainly foreign. The thought of an African scone is quite appealing.

Alas, I am called away to oversee my packing. Percy finds seventeen valises somewhat cumbersome. Oh, how he grumbles!

Your nearest, dearest relation,
Auntie Cordillia

A Fly in the Ointment

5 December
Dearest Basty,

I have some alarming news! Yesterday I sent Percy to post a letter to Millicent Toastworthy in an effort to dissuade her brood from another visit. Whilst traveling towards towne, poor Percy was molested by two ruthless beasts. After Manfred tended to his wounds, she discovered that the two menacing creatures belonged to the latest addition to Butterbooke, none other than our neighbour, the infamous Dr. Basil Carlisle!

The Rector hinted that perhaps the attack was premeditated in its design, for Dr. Carlisle is notorious for such aggressions. Apparently, he has been shunned from a multitude of towneships up and down the English coast.

Percy requires constant attention, and I insisted on assuming Manfred's place beside poor Percy's attic cot, applying his various ointments, liniments, balms, and creams nightly on the affected area. This has proved a challenge, considering my own persistent ailments of flutterings, vapours, fantods, and wooziness.

I fear that our holiday to Brighton may be delayed, for no other can tend to my personal effects like poor Percy. I trust no other man-servant. As for that brute Dr. Carlisle, I am soon off to confront him this very afternoon.

He shall know not to interfere with the likes of
Countess Cordillia Honeyknob Pryme!

Most displeased,

Your aunt,

the Countess Cordillia

Honeyknob Pryme

9 December
Dear Aunt C,

Imagine my horror! Poor Percy! How perfectly ghastly! When I return to Butterbrooke, I will pay a little visit to that vile Dr. Carlisle and give him a tongue-lashing he will not soon forget. I will then probe him for answers as to why he would have the temerity to sanction such a savage attack.

You are noble and a credit to the Queen in your selflessness in confining Manfred to the kitchen whilst you attend to your beloved Percy.

I recommend a hearty plate of Buckingham sandwiches followed by the largest Pavlova Manfred can produce with her notably mannish, Germanic hands and a good strong pot of Tetley's. It is advisable that you postpone your trip for the nonce. Please keep me abreast.

Your commiserating nephew,

SWG

9 December
Dearest Basty,

I have just come from Basil's, beg your pardon, Dr. Carlisle's manor, Mellon Ball Grange. What a charming gentlemen, indeed! Of course, dear nephew, I had every intention of following your suggestion in administering the most severest of tongue-lashings, but to my astonishment, Dr. Carlisle was all a gracious host should be.

For you see, not fifteen paces from his front façade, the vapours once again took hold. My darling boy, your aunt fell unconscious with only the memory of two vicious monsters bounding towards me. You can imagine my fright as I swooned into an unknown abyss. But, alas, my frame did not touch the well-manicured lawn but fell into the arms of Dr. Carlisle!

After several glasses of sherry and Dr. Carlisle's persistent oriental revival techniques, I was restored. I cannot begin to recount the manner of topics we discussed that afternoon, evening, and then without notice, morning.

Dr. Carlisle, being a medical doctor of the Eastern practices, assessed that my various flutterings, fantods, and vapours can be attributed to my lack of subterranean stimulation. He suggested a Persian treatment involving yak tusks that he would be more than willing to dispense. I am now Dr. Carlisle's eager patient! We have enjoyed a great many hours in each other's company so that we have now gone to calling one another by our Christian names.

Manfred frowns on the whole affair, and the Pavlovas have suffered.

Meanwhile, Giancarlo, good Giancarlo will not go near Mellon Ball Grange for fear of being seized by Basil's Great Danes.

As a token of goodwill, Dr. Carlisle gifted me with said hounds. They will be kenneled in the potting shed. Perhaps I should have relayed that bit of information to good Giancarlo. *Oh dear*.

And Percy, poor Percy, I have nearly forgotten about him, is still recovering.

Well, my dear cherub, I must dash. I am invited to tea at the Grange.

Ta!
Aunt Cordillia

17 December
Dear Aunt,

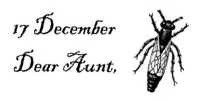

I am happy to read that Dr. Carlisle has persuaded you away from the loom, but I must express my reservations until I am formally introduced to said gentleman. Then I will make my estimation of his true character. It appears he has you under some kind of spell. I cannot gather what a subterranean stimulation is, but I do not like the sound of it, not one bit!

Can you recall that sticky situation I rescued you from not five years ago with Aldous Tixley, the loosely referred to *sculptor*? He kept a studio, if I remember correctly, above Hoorsgate Street. You would spend long afternoons sitting for him, and afternoons would often venture into the evening hours. Curiously, I never spotted even a speck of clay under Mister Tixley's fingernails.

I do not care to have my dearest aunt once

again be the subject of imprudent gossip. Think of the topiaries! Now as the play in Brighton has run its course, I shall return to Butterbrooke immediately to set things as they should be. Manfred in the kitchen, you at the loom, and Giancarlo in the potting shed.

Disparagingly but caringly,

Basty

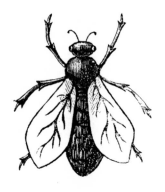

Subterranean Stimulations

21 December
Dearest Basty,

Please forgive my absence as your faithful correspondent. What a time I have had with the dashing Dr. Carlisle. We have been enjoying a motor coach holiday, traveling hither and thither, exploring the country lanes. What a delightful contraption, the motor coach! Basil, in his goggles and leather bombardier jacket, is everything a gentleman should be. And you know my affection for slim whiskers. Why, the promise of slim whiskers nearly had me transfer Percy's duties to Manfred until we made our … well … discovery of Manfred's true disposition. Basil's moustache is exceedingly becoming that even Manfred is set to coveting. Despite being nearly strangled in my scarf that I loomed particularly for motor coach travel, what a lovely time we have had.

May I breech my highly esteemed modesty and disclose that it has become readily apparent that Basil is quite fond of me? And dare I scribe it? I believe the sentiment is mutual. Although, these felicitous feelings are not shared amongst the servants. My, how they glower!

Percy continues his grumbling, tending to my effects whilst he follows in the buggy. Giancarlo, good Giancarlo has yet to leave the potting shed. I wonder how he manages with the Danes. And Manfred single-mindedly tends to her hirsute lip when not concocting Pavlovas. Even the Rector, ever so accommodating, cannot conceal his irritation at the whole matter. I do not blame him. It has been weeks since he last confessed me. I am afraid that my attentions are directed elsewhere as of late. It simply cannot be helped. Why, even my consumption of Pavlovas has been reduced to a mere six a day.

Basil's subterranean stimulations have done me an ocean of good. I feel as if I am a new Countess, as my posture has improved perceptively. Well, my little imp, I hear the motor coach approaching. I must not linger, for the engine crank is cumbersome to turn and upsets my frock most curiously. Until we meet again.

Be good!
Aunt
Cordillia

25 December

Darling Aunt Cordillia,

Before I pay a visit to Butterbrooke, I have decided to make a brisk stopover at my well-appointed townehome on Back Passage Lane. I met a charming young man on the train by the name of Colin Gropewell, and he has an antique shoppe on Lower Swell Mews, not far from here. Cols, as he prefers to be known, is formerly of Crotch Crescent, Oxfordshire. His shoppe is provisioned with various curios that he thought might interest me. He was spot on.

But this diversion should only be momentary. I will be arriving at Butterbrooke this Saturday to suss out this so-called Dr. Carlisle.

I cannot abide anyone leading my dearest aunt down the garden path and then into a secluded wooded area. Only to be … and left for …

I suspected as much that he was slim mustachioed!

Please install Manfred in the kitchen and ensure she engages the local fresh-fruit purveyor. This occasion calls for billows of Pavlovas to fortify me. I presume Percy is fit enough to carry my valises especially commissioned by that Parisian *couturier*. I believe he goes by the name Vuitton. Until I arrive … Happy Yuletide!

Tra and might I add la!

Sebastian

31 December

Dear Aunt C,

My worst fears are confirmed. Whilst in towne, I embarked on research of my own regarding the art of subterranean stimulation. It is recorded that many a woman has been questionably influenced by said techniques. Whilst it is known to improve posture and skin tone and create an overall feeling of content-ment, it can also muddy the mind. Dear aunt, do not make me spell it out for you. Besides, how does one spell *in flagrante delicto*?

Your servants are not only dutiful but quite possibly clairvoyant. Even the simple-minded Giancarlo cannot be aroused out of his shed. They all have the best interests of their mistress at heart. I fear the good doctor is after two things. The first is your fortune. The second is unspeakable.

As a skilled wielder of the butterfly net, I

am most worried that my aunt has fallen into a trap laid out by the doctor, and he cares not a crumpet for your posture. Is this Dr. Carlisle of English origin, or does he communicate in the kind of accent from one of the less seemly countries, such as Romania, or Wales, or ... I can barely give tongue to it ... Greece?

Please do nothing until I arrive. With impending fantods to consider, it is of utmost importance you restrict yourself from no more strenuous activities than your avocation at the loom or approving the luncheon menus or corresponding with your beloved nephew.

Merry New Year indeed!
Basty

25 December
Dearest Basty,

I fear more than one of our correspondences has crossed in transit. I found your letters somewhat surprising, but I shall forgive you, my dear. For 'tis the season for such things. You see, my darling nephew, I have news. The best Good King Wenceslas could bestow.

I am no longer the aunt of your most dearest relation, the Countess Cordillia Honeyknob Pryme, dutiful widow of Viscount St. John Pryme. I am now and shall happily ever after be known as Madame Cordillia Honeyknob Pryme Carlisle! Much to my delirious delight, I was most recently betrothed to my dear Dr. Basil. Are you not amused? Besides a Manfred Pavlova, is there any other joy than this?

Sadly, I have not yet taken a ring. Although Basil's therapies have proved miraculously recuperative, he was only able to slip the ring past my first rheumatoidal knuckle. However, that detail shall not abate my exhilaration.

We have decided to honeymoon here at Butterbrooke and of course at Mellon Ball Grange. I am feeling such the vagabond these days. Our living arrangements at present have not altered, although I cannot say that shall remain so. Basil is adamant that the marriage divan be honored. Devotedly, it is honored three times daily, much to Percy's ill-disguised aversion. My, how he mutters! Poor Percy, his attic accommodations are positioned just above my bedchamber.

Basty, I do believe once you are acquainted with my Basil you shall see that your apprehensions are surely misplaced. I do protest, subterranean stimulations do not muddy the mind but incite it. Yes, incite it amongst other benefits and parts. I insist you experience the treatment yourself. Oh, I do look forward to your visit. You shall see, my little cherub, that all is well and could not be better.

Giancarlo has offered to meet you at the station. He mentioned, from what I could ascertain from his heavy Neapolitan lilt, that he has bulbs, I believe he said bulbs, that might interest you. I must scurry. The fragranced oils have heated. Basil awaits! Don we now our gay apparel …

Fa la la la la la la la la,
Aunt Cordillia Carlisle

6 January
Dearest Basty,

I assume that your giddy felicitation at my news has left you speechless and cramp-handed. Do write soon. I am anxious to learn of your progress in your travels to Butterbrooke. You will find that I am convalescing from some minor lesions. Apparently the fragrant oils simmered a tad too long. Do not fear, under Basil's care, I am on the mend.

Faithfully,
albeit a bit crispily, yours,
Aunty Cordillia

10 January

Dear Aunt,

I beg your pardon . . .

Countess Cordillia

Honeyknob Pryme Carlisle!

Oh dear, oh dear, oh dear! This is most unconventional! What can I do but to offer my hearty congratulations? You are a woman of advanced years, not a mere lass. Thus, you will make your own decisions. From the thrust of your letter, I take it that you have established accounts at the emporiums.

I am most anxious to meet this intriguing Dr. Carlisle. Shall I address him as uncle?

Giancarlo, sweet, simple, good Giancarlo, shall carry my bags then. It may prove prudent to transfer Percy to another chamber at this time. Until Saturday …

Lovingly,

B

Butterbrooke Sanatorium
for the Critically Infirmed

11 January
Dearest Basty,

I do hope your nursemaid will allow this little bit of correspondence. How dreadful that you fell ill so suddenly. You have never reacted to Pavlovas in that manner before. Basil and I have pondered this incessantly. He recounts that he did not veer from Manfred's recipe. How strange. Basil is excessively grieved over the whole matter. He sends his commiseration, by the way.

Is it not endearing how the good doctor has taken up the culinary arts? He is a gentleman of many talents. Basil was so insistent on concocting Pavlovas for our little soiree, and for you as our particular guest of honor. He is wrecked with consternation. Well, once you are fully recovered, we shall have a picnic. Perhaps Manfred will reappear in time, but I suspect she is out on one of her usual prowls. Giancarlo, good Giancarlo, should recover by then as well.

The Pavlovas may have spoiled on their journey from Butterbrooke Breeze to the train station. To fortify your strength for the coach ride home, good Giancarlo couriered the first batch. Who would have fathomed he was equipped to bear you all the way to the sanatorium. Curious that he did not employ the coach, as he did drive it to the station.

I have asked Percy to polish my summer tiara. Please do not mistake this one for the tiara that still remains with Charlotte, your actress acquaintance. She might consider her next role as the Artful Dodger.

Well, my dear, you know how helpless Percy can be without my supervision.

Be well, my darling nephew!
Aunt Cordillia

15 January
Dear Aunt Cordillia,

Thank you for your kind note. Yes, it appears that the rest cure treatment at the sanitarium is proving to bring about my usual vitality.

Giancarlo is only too kind. I have a newfound appreciation for the working classes. He mentioned that his cousin, Paulo, is arriving soon from Italy and will be working the gardens of your neighbour, the busybody Prudence Pucklechurch. Her fleet of barouches is to be envied, but I find her piety tiresome. Perhaps Paulo will be just what is needed, for her topiaries are far inferior to yours and are in desperate need of pruning.

Are you certain Manfred thoroughly washed the blackberries? I do not want to point fingers when they should be engaged otherwise, but Bavarians, like Germans, as we all understand, are not as concerned about cleanliness as we are here in jolly ol' England.

Godfrey is fetching my lunch and aspirin, and we will take a stroll around the grounds for some fresh air. If only I could have some stimulation of the subterranean kind, I should be back on my feet in no time.

Your ailing but

recuperating nephew,

Basty

21 January
Dearest Basty,

I am relieved to read of your improved health!

Butterbrooke Sanatorium for the Critically Infirmed is world-acclaimed for its therapies in gastrointestinal relief, dehydration conversion, and exhaustion modification.

Unfortunately, I am unable to query Manfred regarding her blackberry-washing procedures, for you see, Manfred has gone missing.

By the by, Basil, who assembled the Pavlovas for our soiree, assures of the fruit's cleanliness. I blame Manfred and her confounded absence for the whole terrible affair. My Basil would have never had to act as proxy cook if Manfred had minded her duties. Oh where could that lusty fräulein be?

We suspect she may have eloped with the towne fowler. Percy reports that he has witnessed Manfred idling in the back garden, exposing Pavlovas to any passersby. And after I explicitly forbade her near that kissing gate! Her special favourite being that filthy fowler. She would work herself into such a dither that the excitement would overtake her. Percy is up to his nose in soiled foundation garments.

I daresay the fresh fruit purveyor has expressed his relief of her vanishing. Manfred's immodest overtures proved weary to the poor man's nerves. Being a fresh fruit purveyor, Pavlovas are easy to come by and assumedly have lost their novelty for him.

Basil and I had hoped liberal subterranean stimulation treatment would exorcise some of her demons, but, alas, Manfred proved too fleshy for the dear doctor's apparatus. I am afraid your therapies will have to be administered at the sanatorium.

Giancarlo, good Giancarlo, is assembling a search party. That woman, Prudence Pucklechurch, reluctantly offered Paulo to assist in the search. In return, I offered to educate Paulo on the art of topiary pruning. I have planned for a vigorous five-hour clinic in the potting shed with Giancarlo as my assistant, of course. These two will have their hands full under my demanding tutelage.

Be sure Godfrey does not keep you out in the sun too long.

Your most adoring aunt,
Cordillia

26 *January*
Dear Aunt C,

Thank you for allowing Giancarlo to escort me on a physician-authorized picnic at the cliffs.

A great, frothing steed thundering up the precipice was quite the sight. The horse was none too shabby either. T'was your latest thoroughbred, I presume? It had been awhile since I have taken to the mount, as it were, but my mare has a gentle disposition and proved no trouble.

The weather was unusually clement. It insisted Giancarlo remain shirtless. A glistening, brown bicep boasts a curious tattoo of a mermaid he acquired whilst serving in the Italian Coast Guard. One does not mind a few tattoos, within reason, of course.

I understand from Giancarlo, Prudence Pucklechurch's topiaries are improving, owning to the horticultural skills of his cousin, Paulo. She is quite the picture of health these days, flouting a rosy completion and erect posture. Yet still, I can imagine her at the hedges, looking beyond Giancarlo, practically salivating with envy over the beauty of your shrubbery.

Meanwhile, I am in London. There is a charming fellow who moved into the townehome abutting mine. His name is Trevor Groans, and, as fate would have it, we share a common interest in the theatrical arts. He, a budding thespian, is a boyish gentleman of twenty-two years but mature in inestimable ways.

I expect to be returned to Butterbrooke shortly. I do hope Manfred pops up. You cannot be expected to delegate all.

Your devoted,

Basty

Back to Back Passage

5 February
Dearest Basty,

I have finally improved from my vapour-ings, fantods, and swoons. Manfred's sudden departure and your recent maladies proved too much for the frailties of your aunt. It has been nearly a fortnight since I have partaken of a Pavlova, and my petulance increases daily.

I am sorry I was unable to accompany you and Giancarlo amidst the cliffs. When you were a boy, that was always a favourite haunt for you. How often you trysted there with the village lads.

As for Prudence Pucklechurch, she was always a vocal detractor of my Basil's subterranean stimulations, but apparently she has enlisted Paulo to administer some sort of crude replica on herself, that woman!

I cannot believe you are in towne yet again. For I feel your last visit was shorter than even good Giancarlo's gardening trousers. In fact, your visit seems as nonexistent as good Giancarlo's workshirt. For you see, my darling, you did not actually step onto the grounds of Butterbrooke Breeze.

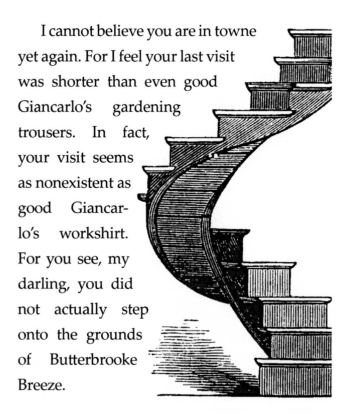

I think I shall holiday in London once I am fully sorted. I do adore your townehome. Trevor Groans sounds like a capable gentleman. I do hope we shall have a chance to meet.

Until then!

Olivia

('Tis my latest pet name that Dr. Basil has recently took to calling me!)

9 February
Dear Aunt C,

I hope it is due to your vapourings, fantods, and swoons that you mentioned Dr. Carlisle now refers to you as *Olivia*. For the only Olivia I know is the towne trollop, who earns her wages at the public house. Aunt, please do not believe she merely serves ale to the local tradesmen.

Once you are fully recovered, I would be pleased to entertain you in towne. My townehome of 14 Back Passage Lane can easily accommodate you, Basil, and Percy. Giancarlo is welcome as well. He can *bunk* with me, I believe the expression goes. With our party, that will of course include Master Groans, perhaps we might engage in a game of sardines?

Trevor Groans is a delightful young lad and far more accommodating than Freddie Winterbottom. Oh, how he amuses me. Trevvy, as he insists I call him, has many talents, least of which is his ability to …

Oh dear, that is him knocking me up now. Off to the theatre we go, for we are taking in *The Aubergine Toast Cosy* starring my actress friend, Charlotte. She warned me that there will be brief exposure of that which will no doubt bring down the house. It would behoove us to steady our nerves, first with cocktails at the Connaught. Ta and toodle pip!

Bottoms up,

Basty

14 February
Dearest Basty,

Yes, let us agree that my mind momentarily left me and that I never made mention of that name, Olivia, although it is quite common enough. I am out of sorts of late. Perhaps Pavlova deprivation is to blame.

Your knowledge of the public house and its *patrons* and *entertainers* astounds me. Yet, besides the cliffs, you often trysted there as well if I recall. I am assured that your intimations are just that. I will scribe no more on the subject.

Dr. Carlisle has yet again left on business to towne. Consequently, I thought to pop in and pay both you and my dear Basil a visit.

You know, my dear nephew, I learned that

the Pavlova that upset you so was actually intended for me. Apparently, Basil made a particular effort in concocting that Pavlova, but Giancarlo, good Giancarlo, trounced on it. So keen was he to take it to you before it could be served to me. Alas, you were the one who fell ill. How curious!

Unfortunately, I was not spared the croup, and I contracted some sort of ailment. We blame the fresh fruit purveyor, why, I cannot say.

Well, my dear, I shall be arriving at thirty-three minutes before three at Victoria Station, Sunday next. Please send Godfrey for me. I will be accompanied by Percy. The poor man deserves a bit of respite, when he is not tending to my effects and sorting my valises. I look forward to my London holiday.

Yours ever so faithfully,
Aunt Cordillia

20 February
Dear Aunt C,

I am relieved to know you are feeling well enough to travel. Pavlova-bourne parasites can be very tiresome indeed. My dear mama cautioned me to exercise extreme care whenever putting anything into my mouth. "Lord knows where it has been!" she would exhort. I do endeavor to remember her words of wisdom, but sometimes I am guilty of diving right in. Speaking of which …

Aunt, may I be frank? Sometimes I cannot help to ponder if Basil has your best interests at heart. Whilst in towne, perhaps you should consult my solicitor, Spencer Twitmire, Esq.

But that matter aside, I do look forward to seeing my dear aunt and perhaps we can take in a matinee of Charlotte's play, if it is not too taxing. Toodle pip and an extra ta!

Lovingly,

Basty

24 February
My dear Basty,

Your concerns for my welfare are touching but completely unnecessary. Do not worry your darling, little seraphim head with this. Aunt Cordillia has been taking care of herself for quite some time.

I am relieved that we are both on the mend. You are right to be cautious of what you place in your mouth. I remember when you were a mere infant: anything and everything found welcome between your gums. Your fixation was so prolonged that your childhood physician expressed concerns, but it was soon replaced with other preoccupations, and all was well.

I look forward to my journey to towne tomorrow. Please do not forget to have

Godfrey meet us at the station. Percy is only good for twelve valises.

From Butterbrooke onward to Back Passage,

Aunt Cordillia

28 February
Darling Aunt Cordillia,

It was so good to have Giancarlo's company these past few days. He kindly forwarded the newly knitted *robe de chambre* and the tiers of Pavlovas with your regards. I am bereft that you were unable to make this journey yourself. A great thanks to you, dear aunt, for your thoughtfulness.

It was quite the sight at the train station when Giancarlo arrived. The robe did not quite accommodate him, and with armfuls of Pavlovas, Giancarlo generated stares. Not many people are familiar with the Pavlova, you see.

I do not think Giancarlo minded *bunking* with me. He was a bit bulky, but we made do. He has the disquieting habit of sleeping in the nude, which I know is common practice amongst Neapolitans. Be assured that your *robe de chambres* was kept snugly about me. Godfrey has just sent it out to be laundered.

'Tis a pity you were denied Charlotte's play, *The Aubergine Toast Cozy*. I particularly enjoyed the scene right before intermission, during which she stabs the intruder in the neck with a kitchen knife, whilst bearing all that the gods have bestowed her. She is a courageous thespian, indeed!

Regrettably, I will not be able to attend the birthday bash for those darling twins Annabelle and Hortence. I daresay that little Hortence has an unhealthy fixation on me, which manifests itself by the repeated kicking of my shins. I wish

Millicent Toastworthy would not encourage this behaviour in her little tots. This new wave of thought encouraging children to *express themselves*, I believe she termed it, is far too vexing for my fragile nerves.

Meanwhile, Nigel Groans and I are coming on swimmingly. We have been mulling around the idea of a holiday to Mallorca, which sounds inviting on parchment, but the place is simply crawling with Spaniards, who are regular Gypsies, basically. Well, must dash, or shall I say …

Adios!

Sebby

3 March
Dearest Sebby,
you seraphim!

It is unfortunate that Dr. Basil was spirited away from towne to business in the north before we could congregate at Butterbrooke so to speak. Furthermore, I am disappointed that a fantod precluded my own visit to towne.

For you, my dear Basty, would have made an equal surrogate. Well, in company I mean to say. I would have like to have met your Master Groans. He sounds very much an affable gentleman, much more so than Master Winterbottom, and waterproof to boot.

Charlotte is quite the *evocateur*. Knife stabbings and exposed blessings remind me of Sunday afternoons at your mother's summer home in Layhimton Court when I was a youngster.

As you prepare for your travels to heathen country, I believe in certain circles referred to as Spain, I am presently uncoiling Percy from one of my wayward wardrobe trunks. It appears that one of the train attendants had mistaken poor Percy for one of my various trappings and embellishments that often find their way from my valises. I wondered where he could have gotten! Giancarlo, good Giancarlo, and his unmatched Italian olfactory endowments, snuffed him out in time. By the by, what a splendid time good Giancarlo enjoyed at Back Passage!

Well, my little cherub, be well, and mind you do not consort with the likes of Mallorcan rabble nor idle near towne fountains!

Tsk, tsk,
Aunty Cordillia

Somewhere in Mallorca

7 Marzo

Dear Tita Cordillia,

I regret you were unable to make the arduous journey to Back Passage. Women of *un certain age*, such as yourself, are often caught unawares of the vapours, fantods, and other ailments associated with the change of life.

And I am sorry I will miss the annual vernal celebrations at Butterbrooke. All the darling, little tots running around and squealing with delight as they find brightly coloured eggs carefully hidden amongst the topiaries.

Nigel Groans and I are happily ensconced in Hacienda de los Pescados Grandes overlooking the sea. All the staff seem to be of Spanish origin, so their grasp of the English language is rudimentary at best. My efforts to make them understand, "My drinko no es coldo, need more ice-o," seems to fall on deaf ears. We are going sunbathing on *la playa*, which means "the beach" in their funny, odd, peculiar manner of speaking.

I do not expect to stay more than a week here. Nigel must return to the stage, and I must pop around to the club. I have neglected my journal horribly. Perhaps one day it may be published and make highly entertaining reading. Must whoosh!

Tu sobrino,

11 Marzo
Dearest Bastian,

It must be delightful to savor the marvels of the Spanish coast! How you can manage amongst those savages of the Mediterranean, I shall never know. I, on the other hand, am once again at my loom awaiting Dr. Basil's return. I believe my latest wool sea-bathing trunks are particularly fetching. I do hope you like them!

What with the doctor attending to business in the north and Manfred's continued absence, I decided to cancel the annual vernal fete at Butterbrooke Breeze, much to Millicent's dismay, I daresay. She has always counted upon, if not relished, those seven hours of respite from her dear little hellions. But, alas, she made her own bed. She should have no qualms lying on it. Others never seemed to. Thus, I have sent her brood off to the abbey in the Rector's care.

Millicent looked to need a good confessing, and little Hortence could benefit from an energetic exorcism.

Giancarlo, good Giancarlo, fell at my feet in appreciation that the topiaries would be saved this year. We enjoyed a vigorous topiary pruning in the potting shed just this morning. With my regular administrations of subterranean stimulations, I had forgotten the healing properties of a first-rate topiary pruning.

Well, my dear, poor Percy eagerly requires my attention. With the doctor away, I insist he is trained on SS application. Let me know when you return from the continent, perhaps we shall have tea.

Vaya con Dios,
Auntie Cordi

14 Marzo

My Dearest Aunt C,

Nigel Groans and I shortened our visit to Mallorca, owing to consuming much too much paella and more than the occasional sangria. Besides, it was next to impossible to converse with the locals, who adamantly refuse to learn the universal language. I have returned to my home sweet home of Back Passage, and all is as it should be. With Godfrey, I barely need to express my needs, as he seems to anticipate them.

I am elated to read that the annual vernal fete was cancelled. The Toastworthys will have to find another way to amuse themselves. The last time I encountered Hortence, she was pummeling a small animal into unconsciousness with a rock, energetic little thing.

I can only imagine Giancarlo's relief that his prized topiaries remained intact. He does have peculiar ways of showing his appreciation, when a mere thank-you note or a handshake would suffice. Those demonstrative Italians!

Does Manfred remain at large, so to speak? Although she is certainly irreplaceable, I have come across a young baker named Gaston who is not unfamiliar with the Pavlova. Perhaps he could apply at Butterbrooke? He recently arrived from Cannes, where he perfected his craft. I had the occasion to sample his profiteroles, to which I dare confess sent me into transports of delight.

Missing my aunt so, I must dash up to Butterbrooke next weekend. I adore your last creation, but would you be a dear and create for me another striped bathing costume on the loom? My waist measures are precisely an enviable thirty inches. I am thinking alternating stripes of purple and green. Ta for now!

Your devoted nephew,

Basty

17 Marzo
Dearest Basty,

So you have had enough of that Mediterranean heat and the equally scorching tongues of the south, have you? I am elated that you have returned to the Isles. Mustn't venture too far for too long from the Motherland, my dear. You do not wish a repeat of the Neapolitan incident! Not to mention the Athenian episode, nor the Lisbonic confrontation, nor the Istanbulian affair.

But I do wish you would pay me a visit. Of course, Master Groans is welcome as well. With Dr. Basil still away on business to the north and Manfred nowhere to be found, Butterbrooke Breeze has been ever so glum.

And to contribute to my melancholy, my husband's absence and Manfred's disappearance has provided no end of amusement to Prudence Pucklechurch, that cumbersome busybody. She is so smug in that gaudy contraption of a barouche traveling up and down the High Street. The spectacle of it!

I hear her groundskeeper, Paulo, is advantaged to exhaustion, poor dear. Moreover, the monks at the abbey will have nothing to do with the Pucklechurch. I understand the Rector will not confess her with a ten-foot staff. Apparently, in her previous residencies, Mistress Pucklechurch has been confessed by all classes of the unchurched and various alien clergy. The Order fears the threat of contracting something akin to the Bubonic and has thus silently shunned her confessions, but not her purse, naturally.

I am toying with the idea of sending little Hortense to her care for the summer.

The multistriped sea-bathing garment I loomed for you is nearly complete. With so much time on my frail, withered hands, I have made an identical pair for Master Groans. I hope I am correct in assuming you share, amongst other the things, the same fit.

Might you bring along a sample of Gaston's profiteroles to pacify a decaying old woman's unrequited Pavlova requirements? I do hope you will. Until your visit, my little cherub!

Your gaunt aunt,
Cordillia

20 Marzo

Dear Aunt Cordi,

It is not in my nature to kindle suspicions concerning Dr. Basil, but I am concerned about his protracted sojourn to the north. It brings to mind the unfortunate incident surrounding your second cousin twice removed, the dear Drucilla Titmarsh and that cad Llewellyn Splaytoes. She never fully rebounded, did she? Now she is muttering to herself at the asylum in Dorking-on-Thames.

Be that as it may, Master Groans and I have decided to stop over at Royal Leamington Spa to take to the waters at the Royal Pump Room and Baths. The saline waters are known to treat and quite possibly cure any number of ailments real or imaginary, including stiffness of the tendons, rigidity of the joints, and gout. They even have been credited to have a mild laxative effect if imbibed in moderation.

Gaston has decided to join us to make it a gay threesome. When we arrive at Butterbrooke Saturday next, he will display his culinary prowess by creating Pavlovas, profiteroles, and chocolate ganache. Perhaps you may want to take on Gaston as a member of the household?

Odd that Manfred is still missing. I hope you will not have to have the lake dredged.

I cannot bear to think of you sitting alone at the loom hour after tedious hour. Of course, I presume you take a bit of fresh air by visiting Giancarlo in the potting shed before tea.

Must scurry, as it is time for my lower tract irrigation and salt-scrub exfoliation. Until Saturday!

Your devoted,
Sebby

Detective Fingerhinge
Is on the Case

24 March
Dearest Basty,

What developments! Our Manfred has been found! Detective Hillary Fingerhinge of Scotland Yard is here with the news. Manfred was discovered defrocked, wandering the streets of Swallows End, Dorset. Apparently, she was victim of foul play and is now in repose at the Butterbrooke Sanatorium for the Critically Infirmed, your old haunt, my dear.

Detective Fingerhinge will escort me shortly to the sanatorium to see about Manfred's catatonic condition. He is interviewing Percy as I write. Oh, I see they have completed their conference [**Note: Aunt unable to complete letter due to fantod.**]

I hope you will not think it untoward that I completed the Countess's letter to you. It appears the countess has fallen into a state of unconsciousness after learning from Detective Fingerhinge that as Manfred Manfred has reappeared, her husband, Dr. Basil Carlisle, has subsequently vanished.

I urged the detective to withhold the news until you returned to Butterbrooke Breeze, but he was insistent. Now my lady is lately admitted to the Butterbrooke Sanatorium for the Critically Infirmed.

Master Greathead, according to the detective, it appears Dr. Carlisle attempted to off Manfred after she uncovered the plot to assassinate my mistress. The near strangulations whilst about their motorcar ramblings, the poisoned Pavlova that you kindly intercepted, and the latest plot, electrocution by subterranean stimulation, were not innocent coincidences but attempts on the Countess's life. Despite Scotland Yard's best efforts, Dr. Carlisle has not been found. They fear he has gone the South American way. The Countess was struck dumb at her inkwell scribing this letter to you. Dear sir, please make haste to Butterbrooke; we are all at a quandary at what to do.

At your service,
Percy

28 March

Dear Percy

c/o Countess Cordillia

Honeyknob Pryme Carlisle,

Please accept my thanks for your correspondence regarding my dear aunt's condition.
I will hasten to the Butterbrooke Sanitarium
for the Critically Infirmed. I trust she is lying
in at the Honeyknob Family Fantod Wing,
so named for the long history of Honeyknob
madness. My solicitor, Spencer Twitmire, Esq.,
will accompany me. You may set up my usual
suite. It will be no trouble if Spencer stays with
me in my room, as I imagine that will be more
convenient for you.

My poor aunt. How often I cautioned her
about the self-described doctor. This is most
dubious, indeed! Master Twitmire will have
papers drawn up to immediately annul this

union on the grounds of fraud. The doctor will not see one pence of my aunt's vast fortune.

I am surprised to learn Manfred did not fare so well. One would think as a bronze medalist in the Baden-Baden Shot-Putting Regional Championship she would be better equipped to defend herself.

Perhaps you might transport Aunt C's loom to the sanitarium to help keep her mind twined in the present. Oh, this is all too distressing! After this matter is resolved, I shall return to the Royal Leamington Spa Pump Room and Baths for an additional rest cure.

Best regards,

Sebastian

Wentworth Greathead

(pronounced Grey-Theed)

1 April
Master Greathead, **STOP**

The Countess is missing! **STOP** It is feared madam was snatched from her sanatorium chaise by the dastardly Dr. Basil Carlisle. **STOP** My mistress would never leave her loom unattended. **STOP** You are urgently needed at Butterbrooke. **STOP**

Your faithful servant, **STOP**
Percy **STOP**

1 April

Dear Percy, **STOP**

Oh dear! **STOP**

Is that detective on the case? STOP I fear for your mistress in her weakened state. **STOP** I will arrive by coach immediately. **STOP** Dr. Carlisle cannot get far. **STOP** I surmise he will have left behind clues. **STOP** Please inspect my aunt's loom and basket of assorted woolen yarns. **STOP**

SWG **STOP**

1 April
Dear Master Greathead,

Allow me to introduce myself, Detective Hillary Fingerhinge, Scotland Yard. And in answer to the question posed to Countess Cordillia Honeyknob Pryme Carlisle's valet, yes, I am on the case.

It appears that the Countess has either been kidnapped or simply wandered off of her own accord. Nothing has been concluded as yet.

As the valet has indicated, one of our primary persons of interest is Dr. Carlisle. As you know, the whereabouts of Dr. Basil Carlisle are unknown at present. He is wanted for questioning regarding the unfortunate attack on the Countess's cook that occurred a fortnight ago.

Fortunately, the Bavarian was discovered, but alas she was completely unveiled, so to speak, with one glassy eye staring out into the middle distance whilst the other was asleep. The cook's edelweiss-inspired uniform, with its distinctive black piping, was later recovered from a traveling circus twenty kilometers from where the Bavarian was found. It took hours to coax it from the dancing bear.

I look forward to meeting you, and, if you could indulge me by answering a few questions, I would be most grateful. I understand from the Countess's servants, you were quite a favourite of hers.

Detective
Fingerhinge,
Scotland Yard, AP

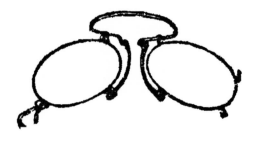

2 April

Dear Detective Fingerhinge,

I am gratified that Scotland Yard is looking hither and yon for my beloved aunt. True, she does suffer momentary lapses of lucidity due to her advanced years, but she has never wandered any further than the potting shed to ensure Giancarlo was earning his wages.

Be that as it may, I am sure you are more than capable of bringing Dr. Carlisle to his knees, which I can personally vouch is not the most comfortable of positions. I look forward to making your acquaintance formally and offer any assistance in the recovery of my lost aunt.

Forgive me for being forward, but by any chance have we met before? Your name rings familiar to me somehow. Did you ever engage in intercollegiate ladies' rugby or facilitate a suffragette meeting or attend a book signing

by the well-known authoress Radclyffe Hall,
better known to her friends as John?

Pleased to make your

acquaintance informally,

Sebastian

Wentworth Greathead

(pronounced Grey-Theed)

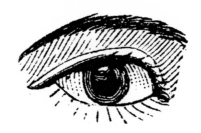

3 April
Master Greathead,

You must have me mistaken for someone else. I am no acquaintance of Johnny Hall, but that is beside the issue at hand. I, my colleagues at the Yard, and every constable this side of the Isles are extending every means necessary to locate your missing aunt. We have received several leads that we are pursuing most vigorously.

Please report along with your manservant, Godfrey, I believe he is called, to Butterbrooke Breeze. We fear your own safety may be at risk, and I assure you, you will be protected in our custody. For you see, we have heard from the abductors, and they have expressed interest in a certain gilded butterfly net that is in your possession in exchange for information regarding the Countess's whereabouts. Report at once, and don't forget the net!

Detective
Fingerhinge,
Scotland Yard AP

4 April

Dear Detective Fingerhinge,

I shall arrive post-haste to Butterbrooke. Please note I keep my gilded butterfly net carefully hidden behind the croquet set that is housed in the potting shed with Giancarlo, the immigrant groundskeeper. He will explain, in broken yet understandable English, that I have it at the ready there.

Have you spoken with Manfred, the lady cook? Perhaps she has recovered enough to the point where she can assist you in locating my aunt's whereabouts. As I scribe this, Godfrey is attending to my Vuittons, and we will arrive this very evening. If you would be so kind as to procure additional detectives to protect my person, it would be entirely my pleasure to express my appreciation to them in a most personal way.

I am of a rather delicate nature, and the

stress of possible bodily endangerment is causing my skin to parch. Could I ask for two of your more burly and most brawny officers to escort me from the train station? They are welcome to room with me in my suite at Butterbrooke Breeze for convenience sake.

Are you certain I have not met you before? Perhaps at the Ladies Amateur Golf outing in Pembrooke on Stoke? I was there in support of my colleague, Winifred "Winnie" Wellwater, who managed a hole in one on the eighteenth, which is quite an achievement for the uninitiated. But perhaps you may be another Fingerhinge altogether.

Dutifully,

Sebastian

Wentworth Greathead

(pronounced Grey-Theed)

An Aunt Restored

5 April
Master Greathead,

I must stress that despite my many visits to Pembroke-on-Stoke, you mistake me for some other Fingerhinge. However, this is beside the point.

I have good news. Your aunt is safe and is presently recovering at Butterbrooke Breeze. From what we could ascertain from the Countess's blatherings, the restraints that bound her underestimated the malleability of your aunt's withered hands, and she escaped. She was

found wandering aimlessly in the notorious maritime district near Hiccups Gill.

Before she fell into a fantod, she named her assailant. It was none other than Frederick Beverly Winterbottom, III! You recognize the name, sir? The Countess's servants informed me of your relation to the accused, and how you openly invited this wanted villain to your aunt's estate. Dr. Basil Carlisle is no longer a person of interest.

Prior to your aunt's escape, Winterbottom pinned a ransom note using a beheaded cameo to your aunt's turtleneck collar demanding that gilded butterfly net of yours. I am not referring to the nets kept in that den of inequity referred to as the potting shed. I am referring to the gilded butterfly brooch that you wear on your lapel and that you are never seen without. Explain yourself, sir!

Cordially,
Detective
Fingerhinge,
Scotland Yard AP

6 April

Dear Sir or Madame

Fingerhinge,

I am relieved beyond measure that my aunt is safe and recovering. Allow me to commend you on locating her. Top marks, indeed!

Odd that she found herself as far as in Hiccups Gill, where many a seaman and guttersnipe take their lodgings. Olivia, the towne trollop, hails from that very same hamlet by the sea. However, I am thunderstruck and gobsmacked that my dear Freddie Beverly Winterbottom had anything remotely to do with the ghastly events! We *were* somewhat more than nodding acquaintances. Unfortunately, our friendship soured after a canoe-tipping incident.

The brooch of which you speak was gifted to me when we were on better terms. If your paths do cross, you may express to Freddie my intentions of keeping the brooch, thank you very much!

Meanwhile, I should think your time would be better invested pursuing Dr. Basil Carlisle as a person of incredible interest.

Please tell my aunt that Godfrey is sending along some reparative Mallorcan Madeira for her convalescence.

Salud,

Sebastian

Wentworth Greathead

(pronounced Grey-Theed)

7 April
Dear Master Greathead,

Sir, I am a sir! Hillary is a sound Christian name of a masculine derivation! I am appalled, sir! But that is neither here nor there.

We are presently investigating every lead regarding this case. More imperatively, there are the matters of your gilded butterfly net brooch, Master Winterbottom who is still at large, and your relationship to the aforementioned perpetrator.

Master Greathead, do you know the whereabouts of Frederick Beverly Winterbottom? What is your involvement with said gentleman? Why does he place such value on a seemingly insignificant bobble as to employ it as ransom in exchange for your aunt? I must examine this trinket this instant! I believe there is something you have not disclosed, young man, and I mean to snuff it out. At this time, Master Greathead, *you* are my primary person of interest.

Good day,
Detective Hillary
Fingerhinge, AP

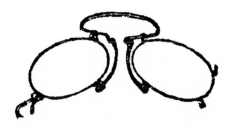

8 April

Dear Sir Detective

Hillary Fingerhinge,

Please do accept my sincerest of apologies. I certainly did not mean to imply anything untoward about your character or proclivities no matter how unconventional they may be.

I intend to cooperate fully with the authorities. Now regarding that "bobble" as you call it. It is gold and shaped in the manner of a butterfly net. Encased in the net is a butterfly encrusted entirely with diamonds. When Freddie presented it to me, it was symbolic of our deep friendship. He, the net, me, the elusive, fluttering, gorgeous, radiant, unattainable butterfly with gossamer wings, prepared to take flight. I do not know the value of the brooch, and as a gentleman would never dare to inquire, but since the box it arrived in bore the name Van Cleef & Arpels, one would assume it is not mere costume jewelry.

You are free to examine the brooch yourself. As for Master Winterbottom's whereabouts, I cannot fully say. He is domiciled in Royal Leamington Spa where I often take the waters, but he also maintains a cottage in the north. Is not the north where Dr. Basil Carlisle was last seen?

Freddie, that is to say Master Winterbottom, is a sweet, athletic, well-proportioned young man of independent means, but I doubt he possesses the cunning to mastermind a crime of this nature single-handedly. He opened a tin of herring once and pondered out loud whether it was fowl or fish that he was consuming. This will give you an idea of Winterbottom's mental capacity.

You are welcome to come round my flat on Back Passage day or night to examine it carefully. By "it," I am referring to the brooch, obviously.

Meanwhile, I am making preparations to visit my dear aunt Cordillia. Has the loom been returned to her? She has little to occupy her day, save for the occasional stroll to the potting shed to assess Giancarlo's prunings.

Sincerely,

Sebastian

Wentworth Greathead

(pronounced Grey-Theed)

9 April
Master Greathead,

"Unconventional proclivities?" How dare you, sir, imply ... but this is immaterial to the predicament at hand.

I am elated to announce that we have apprehended Frederick Beverly Winterbottom, III. It was discovered, through the masterful and tireless detective work of my own, that Master Winterbottom's true identity is that of Frederick Beverly Winterbottom *Carlisle*. He is none other than the son of Dr. Basil Carlisle! For two years, in collusion with his father, he assumed his mother's maiden name as his surname in order to despoil the riches of unsuspecting widows and spinsters. Nobody but I had suspected Dr. Carlisle.

Master Winterbottom foolishly traded with you that brooch for only God and the devil himself dare imagine. He believed it to be one of the countless counterfeits to the original in order to win some aberrant attention, whilst his father, Dr. Basil Carlisle, set about capturing the heart of your aunt, the Countess Cordillia Honeyknob Pryme. Together they planned to embezzle both fortunes—your aunt's, and her late husband's.

When you dismissed Master Winterbottom's overtures and realizing he had given away the original priceless heirloom, they devised the kidnapping plan to ransom its return. For you see, despite his enthusiastic efforts, Dr. Basil Carlisle was foiled time and again in murdering your aunt. He also learned that the Viscount St. John Pryme was a shrewd gentleman, placing numerous conditions on your aunt's fortune that would make it impossible for the doctor to inherit.

The intentions of father and son to abscond with boundless treasures were thwarted. They knew they must seize the brooch, since it would be their only means of future income, and then to see about exterminating both you and your aunt in vengeance. Dr. Carlisle remains at large, but there are new developments daily. Until his apprehension, this case will not close.

This will be my last correspondence. I caution you to employ protection, as I am sure you can easily finance your own arrangement. Your safety remains at risk, as well as that of your aunt's.

Gravely,
Detective Hillary Fingerhinge, AP

Postscript. Please extend my compliments to my dear friend Johnny Radcliffe!

13 April

Dear Aunt Cordillia,

What an eventful week you have had! If only your gnarled, arthritic fingers could hold a plume, imagine the entries you could make to your private journal. Fortunately, I have taken the time to update my own diary with most of what has transpired, but I long to hear direct from you the gory details in minutia.

I will return to Butterbrooke bearing bags of woolen yarn in a variety of hues so you can pursue your avocation once more. At your stage of life, you should not have too many remarkable events.

Better to lean on your household in times of hardship. As for leanings, I have a new perspective of Giancarlo and feel rather sorry for his predicament, sleeping on that stiff little cot in the cold potting shed. I think it would be much kinder if you put him up with me in my room, as the topiaries are dormant this time of year.

Now as for the detective, between you and me, I had a funny feeling about Finger-hinge. I never met the person face-to-face, but the detective's inclinations became more and more unclear with each passing correspondence. Perhaps you could shed some light on the matter when I arrive tomorrow after next.

Curiously,

Sebby

13 April
My dear Basty,

I am making my recovery ever so incrementally. I cannot begin to tell you of my ordeal. Is it not the most terrible of circumstances? Dearest boy, come to Butterbrooke Breeze and attend to your fading aunt. Detective Fingerhinge and his men have vacated the estate, and I require the comfort of my nephew's company most urgently. I am plagued with vapourings of the acutest kind.

Most pressingly,
Aunt Cordillia

An Aunt Indisposed

13 April
Master Greathead,

The countess has fallen into one of her most violent of fantods. She is now in the care of the Butterbrooke Sanatorium for the Critically Infirmed. Doctors fear she may never recover consciousness.

Your madam's faithful servant,
Percy

15 *April*
Dear Percy,

This is most distressing. As her longtime manservant, it is incumbent upon you to aspire above and beyond the call of duty. There is only one way to snap her back into lucidity. Yes, my good man, you must have some rudimentary knowledge of the subterranean stimulation technique. I beseech you to employ this treatment immediately!

If you are willing, please call upon the

good Giancarlo. It may require both of your efforts. Then do try waving a Pavlova beneath her cavity (nasal), as this has been known to revive her before.

Meanwhile, I will call upon my private physician, a doctor of Eastern medicines, Dr. Pandosh Kapoor, formerly of Bombay. He and I will travel without delay to the Butterbrooke Sanitarium for the Critically Infirmed and the Very, Very Nervous. Oh, my poor aunt! What next for her?

Without delay, Namaste,

SWG

17 April
Dear Master Greathead,

I will perform my duty to my countess. Giancarlo is presently fetching the hand crank. We will administer the treatment as you have instructed until she is revived to her former state.

Your presence at Butterbrooke is most urgently needed. I do hope Dr. Kapoor's medical legitimacy is not in question. I do recall that Dr. Carlisle was a practitioner of such leanings, but perhaps it is not my place to question your directives.

Your compliant servant,
Percy

20 April

Dear Percy,

You are right not to question me. How well Godfrey would learn from you.

You are a good manservant in employing the SS, but please clarify, purely for my enlightenment and elucidation: "hand crank"?

I was not aware manual manipulation of any kind was required for this procedure. I presumed it was more of a ... shall I say ... direct technique. No matter, it is important that her aura and chakras are free of impediments, as is Dr. Kapoor's mantra. I prefer my aunt completely conscious as opposed to her present catatonic state, although similar dispositions in her past may make it difficult to differentiate. Desperate times call for degenerate measures. She must be prevented from drifting in and out of reality, no matter the cost. Please let me know when she is jolted back into wakefulness and able to resume her role as mistress of But-terbrooke Breeze.

It is not a supposition to assume that Giancarlo has gone unshaven and has helped himself to the provisions in the pantry. I am not one to generalize about a particular race of people, but Italians are known to take a mile when given an inch or eight. One visit to the sculpture gardens of the Vatican can testify to that.

Order must be restored to the estate as soon as possible. After all, what about the annual May Day festival?

Extend my love to Aunt C when she awakens from her stupor. I realize that presently my dear aunt cannot hope to hold a thought much less a plume.

Appreciatively,
Sebastian

178

20 April

Dear Aunt Cordillia,

I hope that when Percy delivers this letter with the silver service tongs, you will be sitting upright at your usual position at the loom, adding the finishing touches to my bathing costume. You have had far too much excitement as of late. As fate would have it, your name lately appeared in the *Butterbrooke Standard* whilst you went missing.

You once advised that a lady's name should only appear in print on three occasions in her life: birth, engagement, and death. I fear you have broken your own hard and fast rule.

Which reminds me, how is Giancarlo faring these days? I am anxious to examine his topiaries on my next stay. My trip to Paris has been postponed for another time. Charlotte will just have to endure disappointment.

After I visit you at Butterbrooke, I am planning on a trip with my old schoolmate from Harrow, a darling chum, George Beadle. If you remember, you attended West Hailsham Order of Religious Evangelical Studies with his mother, Hyacinthe Beadle. Master Beadle has invited me to serve as his traveling companion to Istanbul. I can hardly wait to dip my toes into the Bosphorus once again. As you can surmise, I will need my bathing costume rather sooner than later.

I pray that Butterbrooke will remain uneventful for the nonce. Next you will be telling me of an actual slaying. By the by, how are the Toastworthy twins? Still menacing small woodland creatures? I shall arrive at Butterbrooke no later than Thursday afternoon.

Your loving nephew,
Basty

21 April
Dearest Basty,

I have mended thanks to the tireless efforts of Giancarlo, good Giancarlo, and of course my faithful manservant, Percy. What a whirlwind of activities we have seen these last few weeks. Your father, Admiral Greathead, is also on his way to Butterbrooke to attend to my health and to my affairs. I have placed myself in quite a muddle, have I not?

He has been in correspondence with Detective Fingerhinge, and they are both determined to see that my estate is repaired. Speaking of the detective, he recently paid Butterbrooke a visit. Apparently, he has taken quite a liking to Manfred, her delectable Pavlovas, and her many other attributes to be sure. What will the fowler do now?

As for the Toastworthys, Millicent made mention of visiting 14 Back Passage Lane, accompanied by her brood, my dear nephew. She fears the recent tribulations at Butterbrooke will prove too much for the twins. Not even the Rector's confessings will tempt her. She longs for a visit to towne, and, in her recent missive, happily considered imposing on your good kindness as you are so fond of her little tots. Well, my dear, Percy is preparing my treatments.

Until Thursday, then!
Aunt Cordillia

21 April

Dear Aunt C,

I enlisted Godfrey to deliver this bit of correspondence in care of Blackfriars Courier Service. I am happy to read of your improved health, but please relay to Millicent that she and the twins cannot be accommodated at this time. It is most unfortunate, I know. The timing is dreadful, but I am having the entire place refurbished. This is one of the reasons I am dashing off to the Bosphorus as soon as humanly possible. Inviting as it may be to take Annabelle and Hortence to the zoo, for there are creatures galore for their disposal, it is a sad truth that I will not be able to do so at this time.

I may be able to stay one night at Butterbrooke, long enough to visit, collect my bathing costume, and leave Father to enjoy his stay without me. Regrettably, I shall miss him as well. Perhaps next year, or the year next.

Godfrey is seeing to my portmanteau. I shall arrive shortly.

As always,
Sebby

22 April
Dearest Basty,

What disappointment! I so longed for an extended visit with my nephew, and, likewise, I am sure Millicent and the twins will be disappointed not to enjoy an extensive holiday at Back Passage. I have always found it strange that they insist on traveling away from Tinkerbush, Oxfordshire. They have a lovely manor home. Perhaps they should spend more time there.

I do have some news. Detective Fingerhinge has just departed. It appears Freddie Winterbottom Carlisle has escaped! Imagine my horror at the news! The admiral has decided to travel to towne to see to my loose ends, so to speak, with the various solicitors there.

Perhaps you might consider lengthening your visit? You will find Manfred's Pavlovas to be even more celestially inspired. They are particularly heaven-blessed when after a visit from old Fingerhinge.

Whether you linger here or go abroad, please take care. That lunatic Winterbottom, not to mention the evil Dr. Carlisle, remain at large and out for revenge.

Happy holiday,
Aunt Cordillia,

Postscript. Enclosed is your newly fash-ioned sea-bathing costume. I hope you do not mind the embellishments.

24 April

Dear Aunt C!

I simply adore my new bathing costume! It fits like a glove, and again you thoughtfully made the stripes vertical. You are too kind! I am sure to generate waves in the Bosphorus! Yes, it is poor luck I will not be able to spend time with the Toastworthy tots. Dreadful pity. Perhaps another time.

Regarding Freddie Winterbottom Carlisle, that is most alarming news. I do hope Detective Fingerhinge has the best men on the case. If I should ever encounter Freddie, I will unleash a tongue lashing he will not soon forget!

Detective Fingerhinge is a queer duck, indeed. It seems rather strange that the detective formed an attachment to Manfred. I cannot help but wonder if something other than Pavlovas whetted his appetite. There is something odd about Fingerhinge, but I cannot put my finger on it.

As if a visit with my beloved aunt were not enticement enough, you dangle Manfred's Pavlovas beneath my aquiline nose, and, not to mention the Carlisles desiring my head on a platter, I have no recourse but to extend my visit to Butterbrooke!

Until my arrival, kiss, kiss . . .
Basty

1 May
Dearest Nephew,

I am most pleased that you are fond of your new sea bathing costume. How I toiled in my feeble state. Conveniently, I have Percy to act as my dress form. I have had similar bathing costume requests for the Toastworthy tots when I made mention to Millicent of your plans for the Bosphorus seas.

Eager for a holiday, since it was decided to postpone May Day festivities until June, she is considering the Toastworthy clan should join you and your companions. A May Day in June defies convention, but what better way to thwart the Toastworthys and play to Pryme eccentricities?

Milicent mentioned Freddie Winterbottom, but I corrected her on that point. Master Winterbottom is the gentleman who wishes you dead, whilst your new cohort is Master Beadle. Is that correct, darling? My, it is a challenge sorting your social circles.

There is no news of the whereabouts of Master Winterbottom or his father, the wicked Dr. Carlisle. It is with great relief, your father, Admiral Greathead, assures me that my estate is intact. He is going to remain in towne for the summer and may not travel to Butterbrooke until the autumn. 'Tis a pity, for the Pavlovas have never tasted better. And Giancarlo, good Giancarlo, has done such wonders with the topiaries. I may never allow Hortence and Annabelle on the grounds again.

Reclaiming what once was,

Aunt Cordillia

An Ayr Affair

4 May

Dear Aunt Cordillia,

Greetings from Istanbul! Enclosed is a photograph of the view from my suite at the Grande Byzantium overlooking the blue Bosphorus. It is but a short walk down the hill to a secluded beach where I waded in the new bathing costume you fashioned for me. I doubt very much if this part of the world has ever seen anyone with such a rippingly smart costume, judging from the looks I have received.

The climb up was so beastly that a well-proportioned young man by the name of Yasif offered a ride back via a cart and a donkey. So terribly rustic, these Turks are. Of course, I tipped him quite generously. Poor Yasif does not speak a word of the Queen's English, but through animated hand signals, when they were not employed otherwise, we are able to communicate remarkably well. My traveling companion, George Beadle, is wary of the Turkish natives and is certain they are motivated purely by monetary gain.

I do long for a decent crumpet and a cuppa Earl Grey, since they serve the most suspicious-looking meals here. I should be returning to the folds, no disrespect to Manfred, of Butterbrooke Breeze in a fortnight.

As always, your adoring nephew,

Sebby

6 May
Dearest Sebby,

I am happy to read you are enjoying your holiday, but, my goodness, dear, Istanbul. Must you? Please do take care! My late husband, the Viscount Pryme, warned that Istanbulians are well-known to take unleavened scones.

Following your lead, I am having an adventure of my own. Detective Fingerhinge has invited me and all of Butterbrooke Breeze to Inverness for a bit of a loch respite.

As for Manfred, she has been in such a tizzy. Percy has been more than occupied, packing freshly laundered foundation garments for the occasion.

Giancarlo, good Giancarlo, has invited his cousin Paulo on the journey. It took some convincing for Prudence Pucklechurch to release him. In exchange she will have full use of the subterranean stimulations apparatus whilst we are gone.

I am afraid that machine was the only blessing my unfortunate betrothal yielded. 'Tis pity! Well, nothing like the hearty Scottish mistrals to set my poor soul to rights.

Until we correspond again! Take care not to patronize the Turkish baths, my dear. I have heard that they are overly salinized.

You have been forewarned,
Aunt Cordillia

8 May
Dear Aunt C,

My, it sounds as if you will have your arthritic hands full, what with Fingerhinge, Manfred, Giancarlo, and Paulo. I fear you will have little time for the loom.

Careful not to overdo, dear aunt, as the nearest sanitarium is in Aberdeen and not very progressive. I understand they still bleed, and, with your frequent courses of subterranean stimulations, it would be a must to avoid. I look forward to your next posting before my return to Back Passage.

Perhaps when you return, you will be able to complete the first Communion bonnets for the Toastworthy twins. Is Hortence committing the seven deadly sins to memory or just merely committing them? The dear little thing.

Corpus Domini nostri Jesu

Christi custodiat animam tuam

in vitam aeternam,

Basty

10 May
Dearest Nephew,

I refuse to loom anything for those Toastworthy twins. The other day Millicent arrived with her brood, unannounced as usual. My topiaries fared worse than my nerves. There is something quite disturbing about that Hortence and her enmity toward shrubbery.

Quite by their own encouragement, the hounds have set to her. I daresay those dear beasts are another unforeseen blessing, brought to me by means of my unfortunate betrothal. The hounds' unabating voraciousness has afforded me a great deal of pleasure, in particular, the sight of fangs on pinafore hems.

When you tire of the Bosphorus, I do hope you shall join us here at Inverness. What a time we are having in loch country! We have picnicked nearly every day, and Manfred has truly outdone herself with Pavlovas. Detective Fingerhinge is veritably consumed in ecstasy. However, that might just have been dyspepsia. Nonetheless, neither the detective nor the rest of the party is in want for anything.

Well, my little cherub, please do consider altering your travel plans. Back Passage can spare you until you insert yourself back into the regular routine by at least a fortnight.

Missing you dreadfully,
Aunt Cordillia

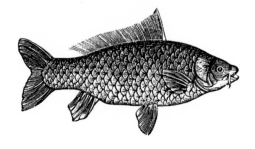

12 *May*
Dear Aunt C,

Yes, I would love to join my dear aunt in Scotland! I have booked first-class passage on the express liner from Istanbul to Inverness. And although I enjoy a leisurely rambling, you know, dear aunt, there are times when one favors expediency over elongation.

I should arrive the day after next, barring any unforeseen weather conditions. There is one port of call in Lisbon for refueling and for the collecting and depositing of Lisbonites, or is it Lisbonians, or Lisberanians? You can never be too sure. But they are undoubtedly Portuguese.

Curious that Manfred's Pavlovas have grown exponentially since Fingerhinge has arrived on the scene. I suppose the golfing season is likewise in full bloom. I know your cottage in Inverness is cozier than Butterbrooke; therefore, if it requires that I *bunk* with Giancarlo and Paulo, I will "rough it," as they say. My father, the admiral, raised me to be a Spartan soldier, as it were. I hope Giancarlo and Paulo packed their rods for the lochs. I can almost taste the catch of the day now!

When George Beadle confirmed that Istanbulians can be quite motivated by monetary inducements to provide all manner of succor, he decided to remain on, thankfully, I might add. He has grown quite tiresome.

Please have Percy meet Godfrey and me at the docks at thirty minutes after one in the afternoon. I can only stay but a week, then

I must sally forth to Back Passage. It is the annual swearing-in ceremony at the Ramsbottom Drinking Club. I expect to see some old chums from my days at Queen's College. True, I never studied there, but I did act as an artist's model for a term or two.

As ever,

Basty

14 May
Dearest Basty,

What a treat if you will be able to join us! But dearest, please book passage to Ayr. Upon Detective Fingerhinge's suggestion, our party has decided to travel to the birthplace of golf and the infamous marmot refuge. My favourite is the North American Hoary Marmot. The first of those furry creatures were shipped from the colonies in the late eighteenth century and whose reproductive habits rival that of a Toastworthy.

Fingerhinge is quite the aficionado of golf, apparently. He once played for the league, or something of that sort. They are quite cliquish, those leagues.

I believe you will find the accommodations

at Ayr most palatial. Therefore, there will be no need of "roughing it."

Giancarlo and his cousin Paulo made mention of a nature retreat in the bogs that may interest you, knowing what an appreciator of all things natural you are. What size Wellingtons do you take, my dear?

Oh, what diversion is to be had at Ayr! Days of picnicking on the coast and nights orating Robert Burns by firelight. 'Tis a shame that Master Beadle will not be joining you. However, any guest of yours is welcome. I can never keep abreast of your acquaintances, my dear.

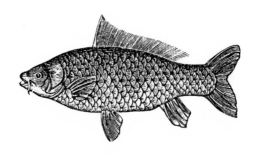

Wait until I reveal my latest loomed project, a kilt of such splendour! I believe it is my best work. Detective Fingerhinge made a special request for the garment. It will compliment his sturdy appendages nicely.

See you there at Ayr,
Aunt Cordillia

16 May
Dear Aunt Cordi,

I hear there's no air that compares to air in Ayr. I am not much of a sportsman like Fingerhinge but will happily offer my most sincere golf clap as he whacks the little balls. I hope you loomed his, or should I say her, kilt in the Radclyffe tartan, of which her ancestors once tilled the fields, thus the propensity for thick ankles and broad shoulders, even in the fairer sex. Not everyone can pull off a kilt, and I know better than most.

Perhaps Giancarlo and I will amuse ourselves by truffle hunting in the bogs. The Toastworthys are coming 'round, are they? And just as my shins have finally healed.

If I may impose on Manfred, I speak culinarily, of course, but I understand she is up to her elbows entertaining the detective at the moment.

Rather peckish,

Basty

18 May
Dearest Bastian,

Giancarlo, good Giancarlo is quite keen on the idea of truffle hunting with you, if you do not mind the addition of his cousin, Paulo. And speaking of Paulo, that dreadful woman, Prudence Pucklechurch, concerned of not having her trusty grounds-keeper at her side, has wormed herself an invitation!

And you mentioned the Toastworthys. Despite my best efforts, alas, I could not compete with Millicent's insistence. Yes, they will be joining us in Ayr with Annabelle and Hortence in tow.

Thankfully, in preparation for their visit, I did bring the hounds to attend to the twins' comfort. The notion of the Toastworthys' presence has seemingly chased your father, the

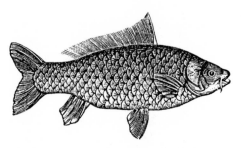

Admiral, from spending his holiday amongst the Scottish heather. I have spent my hours venting at the loom at his absence.

I think you will like the Radclyffe kilt I composed for the detective. However, you must take care not to refer to him in the feminine. Percy made that mistake yesterday and is still soaking in a sitz bath.

As for Detective Fingerhinge, he has been disturbed of late. There is news that the Carlisles may be in country. He fears skulduggery is afoot. For the sake of large numbers, I almost welcome the Toastworthys as additions to our party. *Human shield* comes to mind.

Please make haste to Ayr. It has been ever so dull without you, my little cherub. Once Percy is himself again, I will position him ever so gingerly at the station to await your arrival.

With great expectations,
Aunt Cordillia

How I look forward to a visit to Ayr. New surroundings, scrumptious Pavlovas, and rambling in the glen with Giancarlo and Paulo has me all in a flurry to hurry to Ayr. My only concern is the Toastworthys. Would you not agree that Annabelle and Hortence would be better suited to the paddock? Of course, they should be under the watchful eye of Millicent. She tends to allow them to run feral in the development of *self*, or some such Viennese rot.

I suspect it was little Hortence herself who gifted me with an asp the last visit. At first, I notioned that perhaps Giancarlo was suffering one of his nocturnal somnambulistic writhings. Portrait my dismay when, alas, I discovered it was a reptilian attack. Godfrey has been assigned the additional responsibility of examining my bed before retiring. This will take precedence even above starching my Y-fronts.

I am curious to witness Fingerhinge in his new kilt. Did you not tell me he is nursing a downy moustache?

Please alert Percy to ready one of the more endowed carriages at the station. We have packed for an extensive stay. And by "we," I refer to Godfrey, as I am traveling companionless. Please also instruct Manfred that I expect to see an exuberance of fresh berries and rose petals atop my Pavlova. Until the morrow.

Will repair to Ayr,

S W G

22 May
Dearest Basty,

I have poised Percy at the Ayr train station. Still on the mend, he ran along the barouche. So you see, all your various effects will be well accommodated. Manfred assures me that the fresh-fruit purveyor and the florist are at the ready to make certain the Pavlovas are nothing less than transcendent.

The Toastworthys arrived yesterday. However, we have yet to see the twins. Apparently the hounds assigned to their bedchamber door have discouraged them from venturing out. I situated those most robust youngsters in the highest tower with the shortest bed sheets; therefore, escape is unlikely.

I have been enjoying idle days at my loom whilst Fingerhinge and Manfred enjoy lengthy excursions, "hikes," I believe they call them,

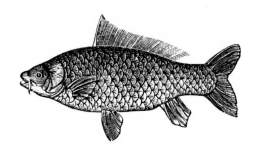

amidst the moors. Manfred recently joined a Flemish-founded association who celebrate such outings, so to speak. I believe they are called "Dikes Who Hike," or some such, but I may be mistaken.

Giancarlo, good Giancarlo, and Paulo are occupied attending to their bronzing, and Millicent spends the good part of the day at the nearby abbey's confessional. No one is more devout than Millicent. It is no wonder, what with Annabelle and Hortence to contend with, one would be compelled to turn to the Lord for consolation and thanksgiving. Yes, thanksgiving. For despite the near drownings, canine encounters, and all the slipping from cliff faces, the twins' dependable health is the only thing she is assured of these days.

My dearest little nymph, how I am elated with anticipation at your arrival! I believe this holiday will prove to be our most successful yet.

Without a care in Ayr,

Aunt Cordillia

Would it be a terrible imposition if I brought along my chum, Nigel Groans? He is a dear fellow.

Thank you for my lovely gift of the tinker clock. It sits proudly upon my armoire, where I keep my delicates and silk robes des chambres. This morning the clock greeted me with the sounds of wee birds tweeting. Meanwhile, Godfrey remained in deep, geriatric slumber, and I had to draw my own bath. Imagine!

I understand Millicent Toastworthy gave birth to a male child and named it Ignatius. My, what an interesting name. With such a name, his world is open to a soprano's range of possibilities, from that of a newt breeder to the Pope.

Aunt, I am concerned. Do you think Fingerhinge is perhaps forming an unnatural bond to Manfred? My fear is that Fingerhinge will snatch Manfred away, and you will be interviewing new Pavlova concocters. There is something funny about Fingerhinge. He is moustached, yes, but, for being nearly forty, it is not much more than a downy growth. It is quite worrisome.

Well, that is neither here nor there, as you so often expostulate. Until the afternoon before next!

I remain your nymphlike nephew,

Sebby

26 May
Dearest Sebby,

How good it is to hear from you yet again! We are fortunate that the post has been so reliable of late. I am pleased to learn you are enjoying the tinker clock, although I wish it would remind you to honor your travel arrangements, dear. I nearly forgot about poor Percy, who remains stationed at the station.

I have just employed Giancarlo, good Giancarlo, to courier over a ham sandwich to him. And, of course, Nigel Groans is more than welcome to join us in Ayr, but, my dear, I thought you had parted ways not entirely amicably on a Mallorcan beach. I have a vague memory of another companion of yours that was slated to accompany you, but alas I cannot recall the name. Like the train station that is serving as Percy's temporary accommodation, it is difficult for your aunt to keep track of the arrivals and departures of your social schedule.

Alas, you heard the news that Millicent has sprouted a son. Indeed, Ignatius, I believe that is what she is calling him, arrived without fore-warning or provocation. Why, I had forgotten the girl was with child ... again. I suspected she bore that appearance due to the unseason-able heat we have been enduring. You know how the Toastworthys bubble and bloat when exposed to the slightest hint of humidity.

We were having tea, and, just as easily as passing the cream, the child appeared. Percy, poor Percy, was overheard intimating that the conception was far from immaculate. I admon-ished him instantly, of course, but for once I must agree.

I have sequestered Millicent and all her off-spring to the tower. I do hope all are accounted for. Perhaps your delayed journey proved well timed, for the scene, although otherwise uneventful, was a bit untidy. Percy is still tending to the mess.

But let not this concern you, my dear. Everything should be sorted for your arrival. Detective Fingerhinge has procured himself faux follicles to shore up his handlebar moustache. The overnight appearance of that upperlip embellishment was the most exciting event we have witnessed this past fortnight.

Enjoying a splendid
Scots holiday,
Aunt Cordillia

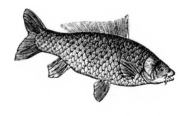

28 May

Dear beloved Aunt,

Thank you, as usual, for your offer of hospitality. I am sorry to have altered my plans. Master Groans and I have formed an alliance once again, and he kindly invited me for a short holiday at his family's summer home on Lake Geneva.

It would have been a treat to witness Manfred in her newly designed white uniform with black piping and wheat tresses gathered in a severe bun. I pray her feelings will not be injured as I will not be able to partake of my fill of Pavlovas. I am certain I should have reached my bursting point, but that is now up to Fingerhinge. I believe her friendship with the detective has rather softened many of her sharper Teutonic edges.

Rather than gifting Ignatius Toastworthy with a present directly, I hope Millicent will accept my donation to the South London Unwed Teen Society in his honor.

If I can awaken Godfrey from his third *siesta*, as the Spaniards refer to it, I will have him tend to packing my valises for the journey to Switzerland.

Your gadabout nephew,

Sebby

30 May
Dearest Seb,

If Lake Geneva requires your presence, your dear old aunt doth not protest too much. But I am most exceedingly disappointed. Nonetheless, I am thrilled that you and Master Groans are on better terms in time for a holiday. I understand it is swollen this time of year. I refer to that renowned body of water, of course. Please do remember to pack the line of bathing-wear I have conjured for you. Verticals cannot fail to flatter.

Manfred pouted for days after you declined her invitation of Pavlovas. She labored for hours concocting them especially for you. Thankfully, Fingerhinge festooned her with a handsome ribboned bowtie to compliment her white kitchen frock. She has since cheered up considerably.

I think your donation to the South London Unwed Teen Society is quite a generous gift. Goodness knows that Millicent herself was two turns away from seeking their services if not for her fortunate betrothal to my good dead husband's dead brother. She was quite in the family way when she lumbered down the aisle. Let us agree that the colour white suits even Manfred better than poor Millicent. 'Tis pity …

Well, my dear, I am presently directing Percy with my own valises for my return journey home to Butterbrooke Breeze. I left a note for housekeeping. I seemed to have misplaced the key to the north tower, and I have instructed them to see to the Toastworthys when it is found, eventually, someday.

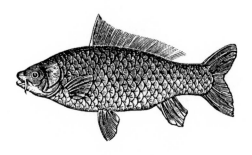

Safe travels to you, my dear. You were always plagued by wanderlust, amongst others plagues, even as a wee little tot.

Yours most belovedly,

Cordillia

A Swing around the Maypole

1 June
Dear Aunt Cordillia,

Guten Tag! I am happy you are returning to Butterbrooke and to routine. And not a moment too soon.

I am sorry to have not written in several days. Master Groans keeps me on the go. Just yesterday, we spent the better part of an afternoon spelunking. The Alps have some charming ice caves to go spelunking in. I have never spelunked in Great Britain, but I am always keen for new endeavors. I would imagine Giancarlo would enjoy a good spelunking, being the out-of-doors type.

Meanwhile, last time I checked, Godfrey was still in his nightshirt. *Danke Gott* for Hans. Such a helpful lad! His lederhosen are as flattering as they are supportive. If it weren't for him, I might have starved. I must dash, as he is about to serve lunch, and Hans claims his schnitzel is fresh today. And there is nothing worse than day-old schnitzel. He is in training as a gymnast, so he cuts a rather dashing figure, as is the general consensus.

I expect to return to Back Passage no later than Sunday. Are you giving your annual May Day festival on the south lawn? I suppose all the Toastworthys will be in attendance, even the freshest one, Ignatius. His teeth are coming in early, are they not? I hope Millicent takes care. If I recall, it took Hortence five years to be weaned.

Might I suggest Annabelle and Hortence should be kept a good distance away from the ponies this year, Hortence especially? Yet to recuperate from last year's celebrations, the livestock are hardly living up to their name. Millicent need not have provided her with an actual crop.

Auf Wiedersehen,

Sebby

5 June
Dearest Sebby,

Your aunt is just positively diminished with these weeks of travel and with preparations of the June May Day festivities. I just received a letter from cousin Pippa Higgswallow. The missive was a total of thirty-seven pages front to back. Neither I nor Percy could make heads or tales of it, but Giancarlo, good Giancarlo, got quite a tickle from the letter. It has been subsequently added to the compost. Her niece, Sissy Higgswallow, is eager to join our vernal revelries. With her presence, that would leave the Toastworthys out, which may be a relief to the topiaries and my nerves (like my yarn, they would likely to have frayed).

I am presently engaged at my loom, my only solace. I hope to have your progressively fashioned cape completed in a fortnight.

Please extend my greetings to Master Groans and Herr Hans. Be careful not to consume too much knackwurst, my love. It took months for you to recover from that contest. Perhaps it was worth the title of twenty-three knackwurst in twenty-three minutes, despite the dislocated mandible. Ever the fierce competitor, you weren't the wurst for the wear.

Proceed with care,
Aunt Cordillia

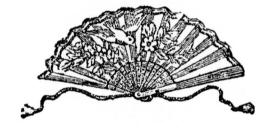

8 June

Dear Aunt Cordillia,

Imagine my relief that not a Toastworthy will be in attendance this year! Giancarlo's finely tended topiaries will remain unmolested.

Sissy Higgswallow! What a charming name! I don't believe I have ever met a Sissy before. Of what age is the young lady? I hope she does not have any disquieting habits like kicking gentlemen in the shins or bludgeoning small animals with a croquet mallet. Self-expression is quite overrated and need not always be tolerated or condoned.

I know it is not my place to organize your guest list, but I sincerely hope that Prunella Prudeholme, who is a relation of some sort to Prudence Pucklechurch, will not bring her prized King Charles spaniel, Philip. At the last May Day, Philip took too much of a liking to my leg and made the oddest movements. I scarcely enjoyed my crumpet and cuppa Darjeeling tea.

If that were not enough, Prunella insisted on reading aloud to me from scripture. There was nothing holy about it. Between her mutterings, humpings, and thumpings, I believed she was on the subterranean stimulation! Apparently, she believes my soul requires saving from a life of leisure and earthly pursuits. But, Aunt, I put to you, what life is worth living without leisure and earthly pursuits? There is nothing more fatiguing than being witnessed to. My apologies, dear aunt, but I find it difficult to concentrate on luncheon whilst having a rambunctious beast attached to my leg and being delivered from evil at the same time. Blessedly, I found refuge in Giancarlo's potting shed.

Must dash, as Hans is about to give me private yodeling lessons.

Yodel ay hee hooooooooooooo!

Basty

12 June
Dearest Basty,

You will be happy to know that our May Day preparations are nearly complete. And the Toastworthys will be sadly absent this year. I understand from the castle staff at Ayr that following a clandestine escape from the north tower, they report that the Toastworthys booked passage to London, perhaps in the hopes for a visit with you?

Sissy Higgswallow arrived yesterday. She is a charming, plump little thing, just turned sixteen, and accompanied by her equally ample aunt, Pippa. Percy had a time extracting their oversized valises from the carriage. Poor dear, took him nearly three hours! Though, I must say it is rather pleasant having the company of ladies again. Although Manfred theoretically is of the female persuasion, of all her sides, she lacks a softer one that would lend itself toward feminine companionship.

Unfortunately, the Pavlovas have been suffering as of late. Detective Fingerhinge was called on assignment from the Yard. Manfred just lingers in the garden, swinging on the kissing gate, hoping for the detective's speedy return. Is that not romantic, my dear nephew? The Brontës could have done no better. Giancarlo has repaired the gate four times, and not just the hinges but the whole dilapidated structure itself.

With great thanks, the ladies do not seem to notice the decline of the Pavlovas. From what I gather, they are not too discriminatory with their confections and have little experience with Pavlovas upon which to make a comparison.

Neither a Pucklechurch nor a Prudeholme is entered as a guest to my soirée. Last I heard, Prunella was off on another pursuit to the Alps of the missionary kind, a common position of the Prudeholmes. You may very well encounter her and her frisky spaniel on the slopes yourself.

Well, my dear, I must away. The ladies Higgswallow are demanding my attention. They have expressed great interest in horticulture and cannot be persuaded from Giancarlo's potting shed.

Three's company,
Aunt Cordillia

18 June

Dear Aunt C,

It seems like days have passed since I have last corresponded with my beloved aunt. I have been inconvenienced with a malady. As soon as I return to London, I am going to consult my physician, Doctor Albert Hall, not to be confused by the auditorium of the same name.

I have developed a curious nervous twitch in my right eye that seems to be brought upon by strident, unwelcoming voices. I have always been the sensitive sort since a wee tot. Do you recollect when you once favored me with shrieked nursery rhymes?

It may just be that I require a thorough subterranean stimulation. Which reminds me, is Giancarlo caring for your topiaries as his duties demand? Usually he is only too willing to oblige.

The Higgswalllows sound perfectly delightful, but you must try to discourage Sissy away from the Pavlovas. What a young girl needs is exercise and lots of it. Though please see to it she does not lollygag amidst the potting shed.

Odd that you should mention it, but indeed Prunella Prudeholme was staying at the very same chalet in Lake Geneva. At breakfast, she would glare at me from across the room as if I were the Prince of Darkness himself. Naturally, she left me much reading material about the saving of one's soul and the like. And naturally I discarded it in the nearest rubbish bin. Meanwhile, Philip, the spaniel, again made advances upon my shin.

I long for a Pavlova, but the longing will make it all the sweeter when I finally wrap my trembling, greedy lips around one or two or three; each one is its own delight.

I remain,

Sebby

A Staff Infection

4 July
Dearest Basty,

'Tis so good of you to interrupt your holiday merrymaking to send your aunt a letter now and again. Even amidst your various ailments you find the time to correspond. Such a dear boy you are! I apologize for the bit of delay in my reply. Prudence Pucklechurch, after much subtle persuading, has finally left.

Her visit, although exasperating, was not altogether fruitless. Were you aware, my dear, that her maiden name, and I use the term loosely, is Prudeholme? She is none other than the sister of Prunella Prudeholme! I found it quite curious how she was able to relay every account of your activities abroad. Ruling out clairvoyance, I deduced she must have employed some sort of spy. That agent is none other than that dowager Prunella! Apparently, Prunella has made the saving of your sullied soul her singular task, a Herculean one at that. I could only wish her godspeed.

Prudence then alerted me that she has forbade Paulo visitation to Butter-brooke Breeze. There is a vague memory that Giancarlo, good Giancarlo, once mentioned that his cousin Paulo was Neapolitan. However, with his slick, Macassered coif, that swarthy common-man bronzed coloring, and the persistent presence of earth beneath the fingernails, one would easily conjecture that. But, as you know, I cannot be troubled with such details.

Well, the other day he apparently confessed that you were once an informal acquaintance. Prudence may be a bore, but she is no fool. She gathered at once that you were the evildoer behind that unfortunate Naples fountain debacle. 'Tis a shame. I rather enjoyed Paulo as an addition to our party. Poor Sissy and Pippa are gravely disappointed. They have enjoyed the excursions to the potting shed immensely.

My, I nearly forgot that you and Sissy were once siblings in the contractual sense. I believe it was your dear dead mama's third or fourth betrothal. I must ask Sissy which one it was. Two months of wedded bliss, quite an accomplishment for your dearly departed mama. Sissy's father never recovered. The product of their union just could not be lanced.

He and the Admiral were once Eaton school chums, but, alas, your mother always had a marvelous way at divisiveness. Something one can only admire. Now that I have pondered this, I wonder if this is how we are related, but no bother.

Please take your supplements and mind what Dr. Hall prescribes!

Aunt Cordillia

8 July
Dear Aunt Cordillia,

Oh, this turn of events is most flustering. I must swallow, and uncharacteristically this has been a challenge of late, one of the pills Dr. Albert Hall prescribed me. There, my retching reflexes are held at bay. Ahhhhhh … peace descends. Prudence has her facts surrounding the befouled fountain in a muddle.

First and foremost, I did not jump into that fountain, *I was pushed!* Moreover, I was not undressed, as she would have you and the constables believe. In fact, I was wearing a very smart, albeit petite, bathing costume I acquired in Mykonos.

I should have suspected a familial connection between Prudence and Prunella, besides competing for top honors at homeliness. More leaflets have been stuffed into my mail slot. Poor Godfrey just cannot cope! I have found that religious zealotry is a sure sign of incipient madness and should be watched closely. Prunella speaks to me in this odd, condescending, infantile voice tinged with judgment and retribution. I do wish to have this affair put to bed, as is always the ideal end for any affair.

And pitiable Paulo. Banished from Butterbrooke? I will not have it! Godfrey is ninety-three and not quite up to the job these days. When a man can no longer knot a cravat, the kindest thing is to retire the old soul. I am twiddling with the idea of interviewing prospective valets. Perhaps Paulo would fit the bill. True, his English skills are spotty at best, but I am sure he could be trained to draw my bath and set out the appropriate colour braces for the day and other duties as assigned. My remaining requirements can be communicated to him through spirited mime.

I am looking forward to May Day festivities sans the Toastworthys. Perhaps now we can swing around the maypole the way nature intended, and this would be a world of good for all.

Meanwhile, there has been another crime! Yes, dear aunt, a most heinous one at that! Upon my return to Back Passage, I fear that six of my prized finials have been pinched! At last count, I was in possession of forty-five finials. I must put Fingerhinge on the case. Those finials represent many of my travels abroad and friendships wrought. Until they are recovered, I will embark on a fast, and it may involve meals.

Feeling rather poached if not completely hardboiled,

Basty

17 July
Dearest Basty,

Flesh-coloured bathing bloomers aside, Prudence is adamant and will not relent. Paulo is forever banned from Butterbrooke Breeze. I am afraid poor Sissy is feeling a bit like the doomed, star-crossed lover right from the pages of *Richard III*. She has joined Manfred, and they swing in tandem with woebegone visages on the kissing gate. It has taken all of good Giancarlo's resourcefulness to preserve it from complete collapse. Thus, not only the Pavlovas, but also the topiaries are suffering all due to a befouled fountain many moons ago.

Now, what is this news about absconded finials? How alarming, my dear! The price one pays for residing in towne, I suppose. But be of good cheer, we do have our May Day festivities. I do hope the impending merriment will provide respite to this gloomy lot.

The poles have been greased, and everything is in place. I look forward to your attendance this year, my little sprite. With the Toastworthys absent you have no excuse. Well, I must away. I see Percy has tangled himself yet again, despite all the oil.

May Day felicitations,
Aunt Cordillia

23 July

Dear Aunt Cordillia,

I have called upon the dedicated Detective Fingerhinge to solve the horrendous crime of my missing finials. She or he is dusting for fingerprints. Fingerhinge brought along a young assistant who coincidentally I met once or twice before at the Ramsbottom Drinking Club in Mayfair. Small world, 'tis not?

His name is Charles "Bunny" Chattington, and he specializes in recovering missing valuable antiques. He hails from Little Cloisters-Juxta-Mare, which is quite a mouthful even for the likes of me. Bunny has been pitching in, dusting over areas of my living quarters. In fact, he plans to come by on his own time and examine more thoroughly, looking into every nook and cranny.

Meanwhile, there has been an enormous erection! Of course, I speak architecturally. Workers are assembling a five-story tower that will effectively obscure my view of the dome of St. Paul's Cathedral. Many a day, I would pass by said church. Sometimes I even thought of entering and saying a little prayer for my dear aunt and her arthritic hands but was always running a bit late for tea. However, like you always have told me, it is the thought that counts. And now I am up to three.

Despite Madame Pucklechurch's objection, I am offering a position to Paulo as my personal gentleman's gentleman. Poor Godfrey is growing less and less able every day. Just today he paired my paisley braces with my striped shirt. I asked him pointedly if he had gone completely barking mad. That sort of combination would induce headaches of the most profound proportions and would be ruinous to my reputation as a self-heralded fop. Godfrey is ninety-three and not quite at the retirement age, but I must let him go. He is presently napping, as is his habit. Thus, I am forced to locate my own silver-handled, monogrammed umbrella. Please send Paulo forthwith immediately and order him to bring some bangers and be quick about it!

Pretty please,
Basty

27 July
Dearest Basty,

I understand those missing finials of yours are quite dear, but I wish you had not commissioned Detective Fingerhinge. You know Fingerhinge never refuses two things, a lacrosse match or an investigative challenge. Poor Manfred is beside herself with grief over Fingerhinge's prolonged absence. The kissing gate will never recover, I'm afraid. The Pavlovas are in danger of suffering the same fate if the detective remains away. Perhaps this Bunny character can commandeer the investigation whilst Fingerhinge pops in on our poor Manfred? Do consider it, Nephew.

By the by, Prudence Pucklechurch paid a visit but refused tea. Imagine! She is terribly upset over your plans on thieving Paulo from her. She nearly threatened raised voices. One minute in her presence resulted in a fantod of the most phenomenal scope! I fear for my topiaries.

It was hinted that she is mounting a case against you regarding your ungovernable behavior, as she termed it, at home and abroad. She intends to present her argument to several legislative bodies. And you know how they tend to intermingle and can be quite formidable. Apparently, her dowager sister is providing irrefutable evidence of your incorrigible ways. Paulo is someone she is not willing to release easily, it seems. You might do well uttering a prayer for yourself, my dear, never mind my rheumatoidal hands.

Well, I must away. I have nearly completed what I believe is my greatest work at the loom. It is a delightful summer uniform, black with white piping, for Manfred. I thought the new frock would cheer her. Sissy is quite enamored of it and has requested one for herself. Well, dearest, be good and mind that Fingerhinge does not remain in the Back Passage too long.

The finger mustn't linger,
Aunt Cordillia

2 August

Dear Aunt C,

Thunderation! That damnable woman! What would she have me do without staff? Godfrey is more than completely ineffective. I brought *him* his tea and scone today. Should it not be the other way 'round? If I had a farthing for every time I have said that! I wonder if you would consider releasing Giancarlo from your employ? Just a notion.

All this talk of legal action, not to mention my missing finials, has frayed my nerves, not unlike Giancarlo's gardening trousers. I have placed Bunny on the case exclusively and plan a weekend visit in the crease of your ample bosom at Butterbrooke.

Will deliver Fingerhinge, as he or she has yet to present any leads whatsoever to my missing finials. Fingerhinge has lingered much too long at Back Passage, indeed! He has gone so far as storing golf clubs in my closet, which can scarcely contain my own effects as it is.

Make certain the eggs are fresh from the eggsmith and the fruits are even fresher from the fruitsmith. I desire the aroma of Pavlovas to greet me in concert with the scent of freshly trimmed topiaries.

Dreaming of

Butterbrooke's breezes,

Basty

7 August

Dearest Seb,

I did not intend to cause alarm, my dear nephew, and I am certain your staffing quandary will be resolved shortly. However, the idea of Giancarlo, good Giancarlo, leaving my employ is simply beyond contemplation. Consider the topiaries! Not to mention Sissy, whose only consolation is the potting shed and Giancarlo's attentions. And what of my kissing gate? Giancarlo is the only laborer I trust with its care. I will assume that my little sprite is merely jesting.

Well, it is a relief to learn that Detective Fingerhinge is returning to Butterbrooke Breeze. I do hope he makes haste. Manfred has been in such a tizzy of late. Be assured, the Pavlovas have improved appreciably.

It appears Fingerhinge is making himself quite comfortable at Back Passage, but that is always the case. Your hospitality is legendary. Always offering your private chamber to mere strangers. Why, I remember the cricket team that squatted Back Passage for nearly six months. You had a terrible time with the extraction. I believe Godfrey lost a spleen from the whole affair. I had nearly forgotten the matter until Prudence spatted that accusation amongst the litany of your past offenses from her barouche. Paulo is looking ever the more sallow these days.

Well, dearest, I must nip away. Sissy and Pippa insist I accompany them to the potting shed. It appears Giancarlo is keen on a colossal pruning.

Shears!

Aunt Cordillia

Of course, how could I come between you and Giancarlo? Perish the thought! *Please, perish it.* Fear not, dear aunt. Your shed will remain well staffed and your topiaries well looked after. I understand the giraffe head is growing back nicely after Hortence took a billiard cue to it.

The best news! The mystery of the finials has been solved. Poor Godfrey. In a moment of lapsed lucidity, he filched the finials to be cleaned and painted black, thus ruining the patina of decades of charming rust. This may be the final straw. The kindest thing would be to put Godfrey in some sort of home.

Charles "Bunny" Chattington has become more than a mere detective's apprentice. Did I not mention that his family estate situates over the panoramic vistas of Little Cloisters-Juxta-

Mare? Although no scholar, he completed his studies at Lower Swelling in nearby Shropshire and went on to gain a certain notoriety in découpage.

He attempted a Pavlova at my behest, but it fell somewhat short of expectations. I am partly to blame, as I consumed all the strawberries before he had a chance to garnish.

The position I am willing to offer young Paulo has become immediately available. That is to say, not working for a dowager, but rather a gentleman of *bon eleve*. I would double his present salary, and I am willing to bend over backwards to accommodate his style, including his choice of clothing.

Thus, I will tolerate Paolo's unbuttoned work shirts, exposing his sinewy, tanned chest and his snug gardening trousers, not that it is a matter worth imagining. But as it is, he would be limited to the townehouse only. When out in towne, he would dress in the appropriate attire befitting a manservant of Kensington. I am certain Godfrey in his state will not notice if Paulo borrowed his tricoloured velveteen cap with the fanned ostrich plumage.

True, Back Passage offers less wiggle room than he is used to, but he could always *bunk* with me, as I believe the expression goes. I will give Paulo an oral examination on Saturday. Even in his broken English, I am confident he will pass. Prudence may consider placing an advertisement for a new member of her own staff soon.

I look forward to Saturday, when I may enjoy some much needed rest at Butterbrooke. Fingerhinge is fairly salivating at the thought of Manfred's notorious Pavlovas.

With Pavlovas in our sights,

SWG

A Tex Mess

16 August
Dearest Basty,

I am elated to learn that your finial caper has been settled. So 'twas Godfrey's escalating dementia that was the culprit after all. Quite elementary, my dear nephew! Well, now that the matter is all sorted, there is the question of your diminishing staff. It does not become you, I might add. I believe Paulo would be a good fit. You made sure of that whence in Naples. There is just Prudence Pucklechurch and her equally relentless sister Prunella as your only

impediment. Perhaps a well-timed double case of consumption would do the trick?

I do hope you can enjoy a holiday at Butterbrooke Breeze whilst you make your arrangements. We have recently acquired a new guest, a Mister Barnaby Thaddeus Rex, from one of the most exotic of countries. It is called Texas, my dear. BT Rex from Texas, he likes to be called.

Detective Fingerhinge made the gentleman's acquaintance on the train and extended an invitation. With the exception of the Toastworthys, the more the merrier, I say. Poor Percy has been a tad put out. With Sissy, cousin Pippa, and Manfred, fresh foundation garments are cumbersome to be had when a bachelor caller is about.

Well, dearest, I must away. BT Rex from Texas is leading a clinic on lassoing techniques that may prove quite helpful.

Determined to outdo twenty-seven seconds,
Aunt Cordillia

21 August

Dear Aunt C,

Yes, poor Godfrey. I hate to have him committed to the Bewildered Asylum for the Terminally Senile, but it's the kindest thing, really.

As for more urgent matters, Prunella and Prudence can easily find another Italian gardener. Naples is fairly crawling with young men of similar qualifications. One cannot swing a dead cat without hitting one. Perhaps they can find a replacement there.

I am not going down without a fight. I have neither the time nor the inclination to travel back to Italy to interview someone for this position when it is clear Paulo is the ideal candidate.

Now, as for your recent Butterbrooke activities, I am most intrigued by your Texan from the Wild West. Yes, I know the place, as it were. I have often enjoyed novels featuring lonesome cowpokes who traverse the prairie forced to *bunk*, I believe is the term, with fellow cowpokes but for a single bedroll between them. One can safely assume this Mister Rex dons a ten-gallon hat, spur boots, and walks with a pronounced saunter.

I hope he does not consume all the Pavlovas, as I have read that cowboys are distinguished for their voracious appetites.

Meanwhile, I am having my finials de-painted and re-rusted. I have charged Bunny with that dreary little task. My only qualm with Bunny is his fag habit. He barely finishes smoking one then lights up another.

I am pleased to say I have no such unsavory habits.

One fag short of a dirty dozen,

Basty

25 August
Howdy Basty!

If your tactics prove successful in entrapping Paulo as an addition to your staff, perhaps Godfrey might enjoy a holiday at Butterbrooke Breeze as a reward for his ninety-three years of service. Despite recent developments or lack herewith, he has demonstrated himself ever so faithful to the family Greathead, and a long lineage it is. I know Percy would enjoy spending time with his father.

I am sure he would delight in the company of BT Rex from Texas. What an amusing gentleman with his stories of life on the prairie, mending fences, wrangling cattle, and trading with Injuns (not sure what that is). He did not mention *bunking*, but perhaps like Injuns, it is referred to differently on the trail, as Mister Rex calls it. Why, even Giancarlo, good Giancarlo, has taken to donning chaps whilst tending to my topiaries. Sissy deems them quite fetching. I assumed she was referring to the topiaries. I do not recommend them for Percy and demanded they be removed at once.

Manfred and Fingerhinge have been locked in the potting shed nearly four days. With his accommodations occupied, it is fortunate, with the encouragement of Texas Rex, that Giancarlo has embraced the notion of sleeping on a bedroll under the stars.

Well, my dear, I must away. BT Rex has promised to instruct us on the art of punching cattle. Since we are without an actual cow, Percy has been volunteered as a suitable substitute.

Yippee ki-yay!
CHP

31 August

Dearest Aunt Cordi,

A Western theme seems to have been embraced by all at the Butterbrooke home-stead. Next I will be reading that you will be serving pork and beans at the annual May Day festivities.

However, I have my own challenges to contend with. Sunday last, Prunella and Prudence caught me on an early morning stroll in Hyde Park and dragged me by the ears into the Church of St. John the Fabulous; I believe it was in a vain attempt to deliver my soul. Verily, verily, I eventually complied, if only to get them off my arse. I speak metaphorically, as it were.

We were in the middle of a rousing song, "Joyful, Joyful, We Adore Thee," when I glanced up from the hymnal, only to see Brother Ventura at his enormous organ! He plays the organ with great passion!

At the social hour over tea and biscuits, we became reacquainted with a promise he would show me his organ later and give me a lesson. Prunella and Prudence were none too pleased that their plan to deliver me unto the Lord rather backfired. You'll excuse the expression.

Brother Ventura's fuchsia vestments with gold trim truly became him, I must say. It is queer to think his sabbatical from Butterbrooke would find him literally under my very nose!

All this activity has left me rather anxious for a Pavlova. One of Manfred Manfred's finest. I expect to make a trip to Butterbrooke this coming Saturday. I have a stirring to travel again. Following my visit with you, perhaps Charles "Bunny" Chattington and I will take a brief holiday to Cannes or St. Tropez.

À bientôt!

Sebby

3 September
Dearest Seb!

What a delight to hear that Brother Ventura has been discovered! Oh, do extend a Butterbrooke Breeze invitation to the Rector. I will not brook refusal! I shall order Manfred to prepare the most luscious Pavlovas in honor of the occasion. I remember how after hours in the rectory I would find you both lying prostrate on the floor, from what I assumed followed a spirited communion. How good it is to share company with old friends. How even better to lose the company of new enemies.

What of Prudence and Prunella? Did they ever find their way out of the confessional?

My, what assembly we shall have! You have not yet been acquainted with the charming BT Rex from Texas. There is also my plump dear cousin, Pippa, and her equally fleshy niece and your former stepsister, Sissy.

BT is quite a renaissance gentleman and has taken up portrait painting. Pippa and Sissy seem not to mind the hours of sitting before canvas. Considering the subjects, they'll soon have not a mere portrait but a fresco to boast of. Well, my dear, I must away. BT has requested my paint-mixing services. Until Saturday next!

Still-Lifed,
Aunt Cordillia

Thank you for the invitation to include Brother Ventura. He has so few outings from the seminary of St. John the Fabulous. I understand you will once again entertain a manor full of guests, so we will happily *bunk*, I believe it is called, together. I presume you will put us in the opposite wing from Sissy and Pippa. I would not want to keep them from their rest, as often we keep late hours playing backgammon and what not.

I am curious to see the fresco rendering of Sissy and Pippa. If BT Rex from Texas does not run out of paint or canvas, I may commission him to paint one of me so that he might capture me in the glow of my youth.

Our visit will be brief, I am afraid. Bunny and I are taking holiday in the Côte d'Azur. My dear friend Charlotte, the actress, keeps a villa in St. Tropez that she is letting. Her only condition is to train a careful eye on Jean-Loup, the pool boy. Apparently, after he finishes cleaning it, he feels compelled to jump in completely nude. Not that Charlotte disapproves of nudity, on the contrary, actually. But she does feel that common tradesmen should ply their trade and keep the line between servant and guest clearly drawn. Well, I suppose I am preaching to the choir, as you, if anyone, would know the merits of that rule.

If I do encounter Jean-Loup performing something unseemly, I will feel well within my powers to reproach him. It was not that long ago that Giancarlo neglected his station completely, forsaking the topiaries to fulfill some strange appetites. My journal explains the ordeal in great detail and will make interesting reading one day.

Whilst at Butterbrooke, I will have Paulo complete a simple application. I know his English skills are primitive at best and he can scarcely pen his own name, but I am confident that when he sees the rise in salary and the fall of his manual duties, he will fairly jump at the chance to join me in Back Passage.

With Godfrey away at the Bewildered Asylum for the Terminally Senile, I will have to start from square one in training Paulo in the art of manserving. As it is, I must go pack my own Vuittons now. These are dreadful, dreary times, indeed.

Lovingly,

Sebby

12 September
Dearest Basty,

What a lovely time we enjoyed, indeed! Congratulations to Manfred on winning the coveted pink-spangled spurs for hog-tying Giancarlo in under thirty seconds. Why, even BT Rex from Texas was impressed at how little instruction she required during his clinic.

Pippa has regained consciousness. I know you were concerned. Poor Percy may have been a little too enthusiastic with those horse-shoes.

The Pavlovas were divine. 'Tis a shame you could not partake. With Detective Fingerhinge as our ever-present guest, Manfred has been in great spirits of late. Although the laundry has increased tenfold, poor Percy.

Darling, have you been sniffing the furniture polish again? If you intend on scooping up Paulo on your return to Butterbrooke, you will have quite a donnybrook on your hands. Prunella and Prudence do not surrender easily.

Well, my sprite, I must bustle off. BT Rex will be demonstrating the art of branding. Not to fear, Percy has been amply moisturized.

Enclosed is a special sea-bathing costume to display on the beaches of Côte d'Azur with my regards.

Bon voyage!
Aunt Cordillia

18 September

Dear Aunt C,

My apologies, I have been so remiss in my correspondence. I had a minor health scare in which I suspect a banger past its perishable date was at fault, and I was forced to remain bedridden. I am feeling much better now, and, like every sad story, this one has a silver lining, just like the bathing costume you created for me on the loom with your gnarled, arthritic hands and loving heart. I cannot wait to try it out in the Maldives, where Charles "Bunny" Chattington and I will spend a few weeks.

Circumstances have been rather hectic at

Back Passage of late. With Godfrey thoroughly ensconced at the maximum security wing of the Bewildered Asylum for the Terminally Senile, I have had to rely on an agency until Paulo is securely in my employ. The agency sent me a young woman by the name of Perpetua Titling. And from sources too reliable, I learned that she recently exited the South London Unwed Teen Society, the outcome since adopted by a good family in Shepherd's Bush.

I am known first and foremost for my kind heart and have offered a temporary position to the girl to acquire experience in domestic duties. However, she does come with some peculiarities, missing incisors being the least of her problems. Secondarily, and perhaps more disconcerting, are her culinary abilities. She is only able to prepare meals that begin with the same letter.

Just last evening she conjured roasted rabbit, radishes, romaine topped with raspberries drizzled with rum. This morning she came bearing scones, snails with sorrell mushrooms, and spotted dick. Frankly, it is hard to stare at a spotted dick first thing in the morning. Perhaps tea time would be less jarring.

Tonight, she tells me that she will be serve up Paddington pork, parsnips, potatoes, and pressed pickles. All those Ps and not even a single Pavlova mentioned in the lot! As you can gather, this just will not do in the long-term.

Paulo, dear, sweet, unassuming Paulo. If one would imagine it, Paulo chopping firewood unfettered by his workshirt in the glistening morning dew as rivulets of honest tradesmen sweat cascade down his sinewy chest. One might watch him for hours and offer him ice cold citron *pressés* to rehydrate his youthful brown body. He then mutters something in his native tongue about gratitude.

Where was I? Oh yes, I will have to conduct another interview sometime. Come to ponder it, he seems to have other qualities which may overshadow those of a more typical gentleman's gentleman.

En perpetua,

SWG

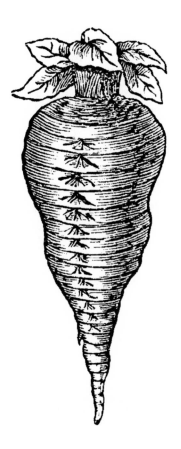

22 September
Dearest Basty,

My apologies for my delayed correspondence. We have been in such a state. Sissy has been near delirium. And, my dear, you are to blame!

Over the last months, I have noted that she harboured a peculiar affection for you, my little cherub, as she leveled inquiries not only to me but to the staff and any passersby.

What hair polish did you favor? What berries did you prefer to garnish your Pavlova? And so on. When she learned that you were ill, she was visibly shaken with concern. Although a sensitive little thing, I did consider it strange, particularly since she has never made your acquaintance.

You see, upon her arrival to Butterbrooke Breeze, she immediately seized upon your dazzling daguerreotype on the mantelpiece and for ages she has been anticipating your appearance at Butterbrooke. When you failed to arrive, *again*, the poor girl descended into hysterics. I queried her about her bizarre behavior, and, alas, she confessed that she had begun to harbour great affection for you the moment her eyes met your rendering on that tinned canvas.

Apparently, the flattering duplet and ruff flaunted in your portrait flustered her. Of course, I explained that any possible romantic union between you and herself was absolutely impossible, because you see … you are, well, as you are aware … after all … you are … It cannot be put delicately …

Why, you are both nearly siblings! Albeit distantly. Sissy continues to be nonplussed and besotted. Percy has applied countless subterranean stimulations with no relief. Neither Giancarlo, good Giancarlo, nor BT Rex from Texas has been successful in persuading her to the potting shed. I have had her confessed, and she appears worse for the experience. My dear, I think it best you postpone visits to Butterbrooke at the moment until Sissy and Pippa return to the Lake District shortly.

Oh, bother, what a turn of events. Well, I must away. Percy is up to his own ruff with foundation garments to launder. By the by, I suggest Master Bunny stay clear of Butterbrooke Breeze as well, for Sissy has seen to it that the saboteur, as she refers to him, would not be welcome here.

Pleasant holiday!
Aunty Cordillia

28 September

Dear Aunty,

Oh my! Poor Sissy. Whatever shall we do? I think it best if Sissy and Pippa clear out of Butterbrooke and back to the Lake District posthaste.

It is a curious thing. Over the years, many rumors have swirled about me as to my predilections, swirled not unlike the taut frame of a whirling dervish. It is time, dear aunt, that the truth be told. Many have guessed it. There *were* certain signs. But I am indeed a happy, self-confessed homosapien of the first order! I sing it from the rooftop of the potting shed! And as I understand Sissy's knuckles often rake across the floor of said potting shed, I am not one to play evolutionary roulette.

With that, Master Bunny and I shall be arriving forthwith before traveling on to Bucharest to take the waters.

Please station Manfred Manfred in the kitchens, whisk at the ready, and have Giancarlo put his gardening trousers to task and see to the neglected topiaries.

I am making a stopover at the maximum security ward at the Bewildered Asylum for the Terminally Senile to pop in on poor Godfrey. His dementia has worsened, and he has acquired the unseemly habit of disrobing in front of authority. It is doubly alarming, since *authority* for Godfrey encompasses, well … *everyone.*

Until Saturday!

Sebby

A Staff Infection Cured

1 October
Dearest Basty,

Really, my dear, I must insist that you postpone your sabbatical to Butterbrooke Breeze at least a month. It pains me to deny you Pavlovas, but we must think of Sissy. Due to the poor condition of the roads, it will be several fortnights before she and Pippa will be able to return to the Lake District.

In fact, BT Rex from Texas has mentioned that he will be departing soon as well. He has been out of sorts of late, quite downtrodden. Alas, his lasso is not up to its usual tricks. I inquired if it had anything to do with you, my dear, since it appears you are most often the cause of much torment. To my relief, he assured me you were not the source of his disappointment, but he would not say more.

What gloom has descended in our midst! Strange, it reminds me that I meant to tell you that I have a new guest summering at Butterbrooke Breeze. She calls herself Hepsyba and found herself with nearly nothing but the striking floral-patterned clothes on her back, pounding at my imposing double knockers.

It was difficult to discern what she wanted at first, but Percy, who had spent some time in the West Indies, was able to gather that she was once in the employ of that diabolical family the Carlisles, who have left her stranded at Horrington Mews in South London. Of course I invited her in at once, and she made herself incredibly useful. Sissy was in the depths of a fit, and this Hepsyba laid her dark hands on her, and with a murmured incantation Sissy was quite recovered.

Later we discovered that Hepsyba is interested in employment as a domestic. Well, I immediately thought of you, of course! With Paulo as yet unattainable, your love of foreign flavors, and my household fully staffed, would you consider little Hepsyba as your new maid-servant? Her skills are varied, and, unlike Godfrey, she is quite limber. Think on it, my little sprite. Then on your return visit, you can just pluck her up.

Well, my dear, I do hope you enjoy a lovely extended holiday. *Hesermaisai!* As they say in the West Indies. Either I just bade you felicitations, or cured you of the pox!

Cuddles,
Aunt Cordillia

9 October

Dear Aunt C,

As much as I would have enjoyed Paulo as my dedicated manservant, it was one of those ideas that looked better on parchment than in practice. It is much like the time I desired an aviary installed in the solarium. Tweeting little songbirds appear charming, but layers of guano proved otherwise.

Paulo is of better use on the occasional, odd job, shall we say? Yes, the idea of having a West Indian in my employ may work well. I am sure she comes at a lower cost and will not expect a day of weekend leisure.

I am willing to give Hepsyba a go. Send her down forthwith. I will put her to work at once. With any hope, she will be able to follow Godfrey's recipes. I long for a good banger for breakfast with my eggs over hard.

Meanwhile, my actress friend, Charlotte, has made quite a name for herself on the stage. She has taken on a manager who is a devotee of the avant garde. Her name is Svletana Lesbinova and was something of a sensation on the ladies tennis circuit until a groin injury pulled her off her game.

Charlotte's latest play will be staged at the Charing Cross Theatre no less! It is called *The Franciscan Sisters of Christian Charity of the Strict Observance*, in which she portrays a novice, Sister Bernadette, who experiences a baptism of fire with a young seminarian named Santomano. The pivotal scene is when Charlotte reveals her contrite soul to Santomano, who then smothers her with a thousand purifying kisses until they fall into a state of sanctification under the statue of Saint Ignoble, the patron saint of venereal diseases, only to be discovered by the Mother Superior herself. Charlotte has been rehearsing this scene over and over ... and over, as she is a committed thespian.

Well, dear aunt, I am off to opening night, and, if all goes wrong, as far as my piety is concerned ... the after-party.

Curtain calls!

Sebby

14 October
Dearest Sebby,

I have enlisted Hepsyba to deliver herself and this letter to Back Passage. I do hope both packages arrived safely. Hepsyba not only comes bearing frankincense and myrrh but news of the immense kind.

Pippa Higgswallow has eloped! And shall you guess with whom? Why, it is none other than BT Rex from Texas! He does not have two farthings to rub together, but since Pippa is accustomed to having only one farthing rubbed, this is of no concern. Alas, he has wrangled himself a cash cow, who apparently could not keep her calves, or perhaps I should scribe *calfes*, together. I speak in the bovine sense, of course. I do not intend to be unkind, but really. Then again, who am I to comment on such things? I have already forwarded to the newly Madame Rex the calling card of your father's London solicitors who assisted me in untangling my own matrimonial muddle.

Well, what do you think? Poor Sissy is worse for the wear. She begs you return to Butterbrooke Breeze for a cheer up. I made mention that I did not think it possible.

I have deployed Percy to see about having the subterranean stimulation apparatus repaired. On his way to towne he plans on visiting Godfrey. That will make a nice Father's Day treat. I daresay Giancarlo, good Giancarlo, is hopeless with foundation garments.

I must away, for Manfred has concocted a revised Pavlova recipe per Detective Fingerhinge's recommendation. They intend to add shavings, I hope they mean chocolate. But, dear me, I am not one for change. Of all things, my Pavlovas!

Please extend my greetings to Master Bunny and Charlotte. If you could be a cupid and remind her to return my tiara. That's a dear!

Cheerio!

Aunt Cordillia

19 October

Dearest Aunt Cordillia,

Hepsyba has arrived and is an absolute godsend! She keeps Back Passage immaculate, but some of her culinary customs are left wanting.

She inquired where she could procure fresh goat meat to roast, and I had to politely inform her that one does not consume goat, roasted or otherwise. Additionally, she has taken to raising her own chickens in the conservatory, which was a cause for dismay. But then she redeems herself by laying out my coordinated cravats and braces.

News of Pippa does not entirely surprise. Advancing age and widening girth are not a girl's best assets, and ensnaring the first male to show any sign of interest cannot be condemned. It is summertime, and the rubbing of farthings are the least of BT Rex's concerns.

Charlotte begs if she may borrow the tiara until the end of the run of *The Franciscan Nuns of Christian Charity of the Strict Observance*, as it is her sole costume in Act III, when, accompanied by Brother Santomano, they go prowling for spilled rosary beads near the Grotto of Magdalene. She then slips into a fantod-like state, and, invoking the Holy Ghost, Brother Santomano resurrects her. Thunderous chords from the piano! Standing ovation!

Curtain closes!

Sebby

24 October
Dearest Basty,

Fresh goat and uncooped chickens! Why, that reminds me of your own dear mama's humble beginnings on that abandoned distillery! Oh, the memories. Well, I am elated to learn that Hepsyba is assimilating nicely. I understand from Percy, poor Percy, that Godfrey is improving daily and that they expect a speedy return to Back Passage by the end of the summer. Great news, indeed!

Speaking of news, pray, could you guess who treaded on my elongated drive in the most ostentatious phaeton and ponies? None other than Madame Pippa Higswallow Rex! All this time, I branded BT Rex from Texas as the social climber, but it appears the young man has a herd of oil wells in the Lone Star State, I believe it is called. Can you imagine! Now

Pippa enjoys a living of considerable capacity. She and BT Rex are breaking their journey to the Lake District here whilst on their extended honeymoon in the Isles.

My, how fate plays her dirty parlor games. Perhaps when Hepsyba is not occupied organizing your assortment of cravats and braces, she could send me that faceless poppet she made mention along with the slender needles. I would be immensely grateful.

Well, my dear, I must away. I am overseeing Sissy's valises, which by her corsets alone is no small undertaking. She will be accompanying the newlyweds home in a fortnight. I do hope they can accommodate her. The lakes are already much too displaced.

Your dowager aunt,
Aunt Cordillia

31 October

Dearest Aunt C,

Whilst Hepsyba has been an absolute angel as far as cooking and keeping Back Passage tidy, she has become devil sent in other areas. She insisted on reading my cards and told me, "Ooooh noooo, Massah Greathead (pronounced Grey-theed!)," I have abandoned correcting her, "Massah Bunny is noooooo good man for you! Beware of the Massah Bunny!" Of course, I paid her no heed. Massah Bunny, begging your pardon, Master Bunny, has been nothing but the most delightful of companions, and his intentions are most honourable.

Whilst taking the waters in Bucharest, he hit upon an idea of writing a comedy for the London stage. It is semiautobiographical and titled, *Lice Ridden Rent Boys*. He intends to star and direct with my financial backing and foresees it running at least three months before taking it to Drury Lane. It sounds like the most clever idea! I hope he can carve out a role for Charlotte. She desires to attempt comedy again. However, I fear it is not her forte, as she received scathing notices for her last attempt. I believe the headline in the Mews read, "Experiment in comedy fails to amuse," or some such rot.

Meanwhile, we are holding an open casting call for actors to portray the rent boys. There are two non-speaking roles for which either or both Giancarlo and Paulo may be suited. Since I have, more or less, privately auditioned them, I feel that they would be ideal in the roles.

Hepsyba also proclaimed that I spend far too much time in a semirecumbent position and must try to help my fellow man. Therefore, I have decided to devote one Thursday a month to the South London Unwed Teen Society. My idea is to hold a class that delves into the means of protecting oneself from unwanted additions. By *unwanted*, I mean that society does not want them either.

I will also call on Godfrey at every equinox and read aloud to him, the poor dear. He is quite befuddled. The last time I visited the maximum security ward at the Bewildered Asylum for the Terminally Senile, Godfrey supported all earlier diagnoses when he referred to me as "Aunt Clara," which is most odd. Beside from the fact I am neither female nor am I an aunt of any kind, his aunt Clara fell off her perch thirty years ago, and had she lived she would now be 125 years old.

A long weekend approaches. Perhaps I may dash up to Butterbrooke whilst Bunny continues to cast for his comedy. I feel I would only be in the way. It would be a kindness if Manfred could whip up one of her special three-tiered Pavlovas just for me. Off I go! Until Saturday …

Your devoted yet famished nephew,

Sebby

31 October
To: Master Sebastian
Wentworth Greathead

My mistress dead. **STOP**

Manfred **STOP**

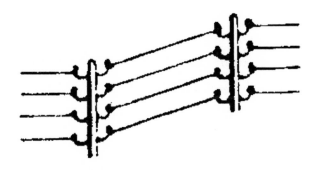

31 October
Dear Master Greathead,

This letter may find you no doubt overcome with grief, but, hopefully, otherwise well. As you have learned from Manfred's telegram, our dear mistress and your beloved aunt, Countess Cordillia Honeyknob Pryme, has passed from this world.

She was at her loom when I discovered her, rigid as her crippled hands. After several failed attempts to revive the countess, Giancarlo and I resigned ourselves to lost hope. Giancarlo valiantly applied a brutal subterranean stimulation treatment, but to no avail.

The household save for Manfred crumbled most expectedly into epileptic fits of shock and dismay. I had only the sense to commission Manfred to send word to you immediately.

Although Detective Fingerhinge was away on assignment, Manfred still had the presence of mind to follow my commands. I believe her strapping Bavarian stock and Fingerhinge's influence are to be credited. But as the kissing gate is again fractured, our Manfred has fallen to sorrow along with all who call Butterbrooke Breeze home.

It has been days since Giancarlo has emerged from the potting shed. Millicent Toastworthy, accompanied by the two daughters Annabelle Toastworthy and Hortence Toastworthy and the infant, sent word that they will be at Butterbrooke the day after next. Detective Fingerhinge arrived yesterday and has set about consoling Manfred and attending to the various tasks of funeral preparations. The detective kindly contacted your father, Admiral Greathead, and we expect him this eve. The Pucklechurches and Prudeholmes have extended their condolences and have offered to host the reception following the wake. It is evident your aunt was dearly loved.

Enclosed is the last letter penned by your aunt. It is addressed to you, as was much of her correspondence.

At your service,

Percy

31 October
Dearest Sebby,

I sit at my loom with wet weather at the window. Dusk has made her secret departure from Butterbrooke Breeze, and the house is unusually solemn. I suspect it is due to your absence, or perhaps I am merely projecting my own disposition on this place. I see from my view that the profoundly bronzed Giancarlo, good Giancarlo, has escaped the thunderhead and repairs to the potting shed after vigorously attending to my topiaries. How indulgent they have become under his virile yet tender care.

Occasionally, I hear the chink of crockery. Manfred has teased us with fresh batches of Pavlovas for tomorrow's tea. The fresh-fruit purveyor procured an obscene harvest of berries to satisfy even Manfred's appetites. That and the promise of Detective Fingerhinge's prolonged holiday at Butterbrooke have allowed the kissing gate to recuperate satisfactorily.

Poor Percy has been relieved of excessive laundering for a time. He will soon alert me of supper, and I may shoo him away, for I have nearly completed your latest bathing trousers featuring your dear, dead mama's family check. I intend on creating a duplicate for your traveling companion. Oh, do send my regards to Master Bun, Fred, Nig … to your friend. I hope you will soon return to Butterbrooke Breeze that I may fit you myself. Well, my dear, I must away. My loom calls to me.

Your aunt eternally,
Cordillia

31 October

Dear Butterbrooke Breeze,

Journeying home.

Sebastian

Ein Pavlova Nachtisch: Manfred's Private Recipe

Translated by
Sebastian Wentworth Greathead
(pronounced Grey-Theed)

*Do not attempt on a humid
day or in a foul mood.*

- 4 extra large egg whites at room temperature. Do see that your eggsmith is reputable.
- Pinch of salt, preferably from southwestern Germany. Never use Dutch. Cannot be stressed enough.
- 225 grams or 1 cup finely casters granulated sugar from the north of Spain. Please note this should not be confused, in any way, with confectioner's sugar.
- 10 grams or 2 teaspoons cornstarch of your choosing, but do take care.

- 5 milliliters or 1 teaspoon white wine vinegar, Italian, of course. May prove a challenge to procure but well worth the effort. Commission a servant to Naples to bring you back a case if need be.
- 2.5 milliliters or ½ teaspoon extra pure virgin vanilla extract, origin is up to your discretion.
- 300 milligrams or ½ pint extremely fresh strawberries that you have arranged with fresh-fruit purveyor
- 300 milligrams or ½ pint just picked fresh blueberries that you have arranged with fresh-fruit purveyor
- 300 milligrams or ½ pint absurdly fresh raspberries that you have arranged with fresh-fruit purveyor
- 1 firm banana, which is optional. If you are keen, Ecuadorians are best. Do inspect for spots.
- Rinse your fruit thoroughly, but not too vigorously as not to bruise. One cannot be too careful these days.

Preheat the oven with 15 logs of wood, or, for those in the new world, to precisely

82.222 degrees Celsius or 180 degrees Fahrenheit.

Place a sheet of parchment paper on a sheet pan. Draw a 22.8600 centimeter or 9-inch circle on the paper, using a Villeroy & Boch or similar dining plate as a guide, then turn the paper over so that the circle is on the reverse side. This prevents marking the meringue and subjecting your guests to lead poisoning.

Place the egg whites and salt in the bowl, and, if not equipped with a strong-armed Bavarian, employ an electric mixer fitted with a whisk attachment, if you'll pardon the expression. Beat the egg whites on high speed until firm, but not rudely firm, for roughly 1 minute. With the mixer still on high, slowly, rhythmically, tenderly, and carefully incorporate the sugar and beat until it makes firm, shiny peaks that rise before you like the Alps on a winter morning.

Remove the bowl from the mixer, sift the

cornstarch onto the beaten egg whites, add the vinegar and vanilla, and fold in lightly with a spatula. Pile the meringue into the middle of the circle on the parchment paper and smooth it within the circle, making a rough disk. Bake for 1 ½ hours. Turn off the oven, keep the door closed, and allow the meringue to cool completely in the oven for 1 hour. Like any self-respecting groundskeeper, the meringue will be crisp on the outside and soft on the inside.

Invert the meringue disk onto a plate and spread the top completely with sweetened whipped cream. Combine the strawberries, blueberries, and raspberries in a bowl and toss with about 135 milliliters or ½ cup of raspberry sauce, or enough to coat the berries lightly. Spoon the berries gingerly onto the middle of the Pavlova, leaving a border of cream and meringue. Garnish with bits of the varieties of fruit and Dark Lady petals from your rose garden.

<u>Whipped Cream:</u>

- 275 milliliters or 1 cup cold heavy cream. I cannot over-emphasize the importance of freshness. If you do not have your own cow, borrow a neighbour's.

- 5 milliliters or 1 teaspoon extra pure virgin vanilla extract.
- 15 grams or 1 tablespoon sugar. Note that *caster* is derived from the word meaning "to cast or sprinkle about gaily." One cannot sprinkle confectioner's sugar. I attempted this once and only embarrassed myself.
- Whip the cream in the bowl enthusiastically with the implement of your choice.

I found that a large spoon works ideally. When it starts to thicken, you cannot help but notice this unusual phenomenon; add the sugar and vanilla and continue to beat until firm. However, do not overbeat! Overbeating is strictly *déclassé* and will spoil the entire dish.

Raspberry Sauce:

- 225 milligrams or ½ pint fresh raspberries
- 135 milligrams or ½ cup caster sugar
- 15 milliliters or 1 tablespoon *framboise liqueur*. Most well-stocked spirit shoppes should carry this product.
- 275 milliliters or 1 cup seedless raspberry jam. Be certain it is made in England. If it is of Scottish or Irish origin, discard it in the rubbish heap immediately. That goes double for Wales.

Place the raspberries, sugar, and 70 milliliters or ¼ cup water in a small saucepan. Bring to a boil, lower the heat, and simmer for 4 minutes. Allow to cool, and pour the cooked raspberries, the jam, and *framboise* into the bowl and beat furiously until smooth. Your groundskeeper may attend to this, as it may be taxing.

This dessert must be consumed in its entirety within 12 hours of baking, or the ingredients may turn, causing extreme distress in the large and small intestines. And by no means include chocolate shavings!

Guten appetit!

About Adderly Harp

Adderly Harp was born in the Outer Hebrides, an only child to British expatriates. Adderly, educated in New Foundland, received a doctorate in the field of semiology. Adderly has long since retired and presently resides in Crete, raising prizewinning koi.

An accomplished rogue taxidermist, a well-respected manufacturer of talcum, and an acclaimed bassoonist, Adderly owns an interest in a string of lucrative launderettes.